Praise for *Revealing Jesus Christ in M*

"My wife and I have known Mark and Kathy Strandjord for over 20 years. I have never met a more God-reliant couple in my whole life! They live completely by faith and trust God for everything, big or small. It was my honor to serve as their Missions Pastor or "Overseer" during the time they lived in Malaysia. As a result, I have personally traveled to Malaysia multiple times, interacted with the majority of the people mentioned in this book, and was present in many of their stories. Because of my proximity to these events, I can assure you that these accounts are completely true and without exaggeration. Their ability to trust God fearlessly in the face of grave danger is truly remarkable. May God use the retelling of these stories to incite others to the explosive Kingdom possibilities when we hear and fearlessly obey His voice!"

–Tim Hatt. Pastor and Missionary, The Palm Branch

"My wife Diane and I had the privilege to visit Mark & Kathy in Malaysia a couple of times over the years. One of our experiences is mentioned in the "Vision of an Orange Building Brings Salvation" chapter of this book. It was an adventure that stretched us both! On the way to the "orange building" we drove through a small town that had the green flags of the very conservative Muslim political party flying all the way down main street. I remember having simultaneous thoughts of what am I doing here and thank you Jesus for letting me be here. During our time at the home Mark shares in the story I was honored to pray for a young family member who was sick with a fever laying in a hammock. Within a few minutes this child was up and running around, these signs truly follow those who believe (Mark 16:17-18). As we left, I was asked to pray a blessing over the family and the village, such an honor, thank you Lord for what you continue to do there!

I have always been blessed by Mark and Kathy's genuine faith and openness to share Christ with others. They both know what being set free to live in freedom means (Galatians 5:1), and they have led many to this wonderful freedom in Christ! I pray that all who read this book would see the possibilities in their own lives, totally free and motivated by love!"

–Robert O'Neill, Deployed Pastor—Hosanna Church

"I have known Mark and Kathy in Malaysia. I had the opportunity to minister with them. I am amazed to witness how God moves in their lives through signs, wonders, and miracles. But what I like most about this couple is their love for Jesus and compassion for the lost. Many have found salvation through their ministry. Their fearless and bold obedience to God's leading will surely challenge people to do the same. Reading their stories in this book brings me to tears. Moreover, their testimonies compel me to pray God will raise more missionaries like them."

–Brian R. Realiza, Destiny Ministries

Revealing Jesus Christ

in Malaysia

*The astonishing adventure about a middle-aged married couple
bringing the Good News of Salvation to devout Muslims
in Southeast Asia through sacrificial love, bold witness,
and miraculous signs and wonders!*

Revealing Jesus Christ
in Malaysia

30 Miraculous Missionary Stories

Mark Strandjord

www.spiritofhopeministries.com

Cover and interior Design: Christy Day, Constellation Book Design
Cover art by: Photo 28776083 / Malaysia Landscape © Iakov Kalinin | Dreamstime.com; Photo 37091128 / Christ © Ig0rzh | Dreamstime.com

ISBN (paperback): 979-8-9861239-0-5
ISBN (ebook): 979-8-9861239-1-2

Printed in the United States of America

I dedicate this book to Jesus Christ, my Lord, and Savior. He alone brought me from a child of darkness to a child of light. In Jesus, I have found a virtuous life overflowing with joy and peace. Also, I dedicate this book to my wife, Kathy. She's my mentor and best friend who has stood with me through many trials and troubles. Finally, I dedicate this book to all the missionaries who sacrificed much to bring others the Good News of Salvation.

Contents

Preface

Kathy and I have engaged in cross-cultural evangelism for over thirty years. We have led Muslims, Hindus, Jews, Satanists, Witch Doctors, and others to salvation in Jesus Christ from over a dozen nations. Moreover, we have discipled many who have discipled others. Currently, some of our disciples have large ministries in dangerous regions. Their success is our reward!

I wrote this book to glorify God. Additionally, to inspire a deep desire to seek more of God. Furthermore, to encourage anyone who reads these stories, they can do the same works, regardless of age, gender, race, education, or experience (see John 14:12).

When we made an announcement that Jesus was calling us to be His ambassadors in Malaysia, we received a truckload of negativity. "You are too old." "You are the wrong skin color." "The Malay hate Americans." "It is against the law in Malaysia to evangelize Muslims; you will be killed." "You do not have proper training." "You are abandoning your family, and so on." My response, "If Jesus appointed us, He would anoint us for success. Moreover, wisdom will prove itself in its fruit. We believe we are following Jesus to Malaysia!"

Hearing from God clearly is vital for missions. In Christ, our imaginations are sanctified by the Holy Spirit. So, when we ask God for wisdom from above, we should believe He spoke and not be double minded.

Frequently, God called us to do bizarre and dangerous acts. Because we had confidence God spoke to us, we eagerly obeyed. Consequently, Muslims, Buddhists, Hindus, and other faiths found salvation, miraculous healing, and divine peace. In these stories, I share how God spoke to us through visions, dreams, promptings, scripture, and nature.

Introduction

In 2003, while I was in Malaysia, I discovered Jesus had virtually no witnesses to the Malay Muslims. Overcome with grief and compassion, I bitterly wept!

I went to Malaysia with a group from my church in Minnesota to encourage the missionaries we supported. While meeting with missionary leaders, I asked them, "How do you share the gospel with Muslims?" "We don't, it's illegal to evangelize Muslims in Malaysia, and we don't want to break their laws," they responded sheepishly. I was deeply saddened by their lack of faith and courage. After thirty years of mission work, they had no disciples.

I left that meeting, went outside, and cried out, "Lord, where are your workers? Fear has shut the mouths of the missionaries; they refuse to share the Gospel of Salvation with the Muslims. The Muslims will never know about your amazing grace and loving forgiveness unless you send bold, obedient workers." God replied, "I am sending you and Kathy to be my witnesses. Sell your house and all your belongings and move to Malaysia. I brought you to Malaysia to show you these things."

My mind raced, "Did God really speak to me? I'm too old for this type of mission. Our family would be furious if we sold everything and moved to Malaysia. Besides, Kathy would never agree to embark on such a dangerous endeavor." Doubt consumed me! Knowing my thoughts, God said gently, "Abraham and Moses were 80 years old when I sent them; you are still young. Don't worry about Kathy; I will give her peace to go.

Beautifully, God replaced doubt with belief and a deep desire to obey. It was a surreal encounter. Consequently, not only multitudes of Muslims found salvation, but also Buddhists, Hindus, and those of other faiths.

1

Disclosure!

I have given pseudo names to those we met to protect their identities in this book. I have also done the same for the villages and cities they live for the same reason. Our mission work in Malaysia is perilously dangerous; many have died for belonging to Jesus. Not wanting to endanger anyone's life, I wrestled with writing this book for many years. However, recently, God has compelled and inspired me to pen these stories. I believe Jesus wants to encourage a new generation of believers to be His bold ambassadors. Those who are not intimidated by their weakness nor silenced by the fear of death.

God Confirms Our
Calling to Malaysia

In 2005, God called Kathy and me to bring the gospel of Jesus Christ to Muslims in Malaysia. Though we were eager and excited to obey God's calling, we needed a powerful confirmation to remove all uncertainty. Evangelizing Muslims in Malaysia is illegal and extremely dangerous. Harboring any measure of doubt would hinder our faith, weaken our resolve, and hamper our efforts. Moreover, many challenges needed to be resolved before obeying God's calling.

Selling our house and possessions to move to Malaysia was not disconcerting. We relished the undertaking of a new adventure. However, leaving our family was deeply troublesome. With our children getting married and grandchildren on the way, we knew our family would not be supportive. Also, Kathy's mother was suffering from an incurable disease; leaving her would be extraordinarily painful. Moreover, we knew family and friends would question our sanity, knowing the dangers of our mission. We needed a miraculous confirmation from God for reassurance.

Knowing our uncertainty, God said, "Go on a short-term mission trip to Kelantan, Malaysia. There, I will confirm your 'calling' through miraculous signs and wonders." Kelantan is the most militant Islamic State in Malaysia. They have harsh laws with brutal penalties for those who evangelize Muslims. God asked us to do a 'mission impossible!' We knew our success would only be by God's Spirit and not our abilities. Subsequently, our success would be a powerful confirmation God was calling us to Malaysia.

We asked three close friends who we trusted to join us. They had proven themselves to be effective missionaries in dangerous regions and were not afraid to die. They jumped on the opportunity to join us on this dangerous mission.

I brought a map of Kelantan, a northern Malaysian State by the Thailand border. While flying over the Pacific Ocean to Malaysia, I asked God to give me an impression of what city He wanted us to visit. God replied, "Mark, you won't find the city on the map; you will find the name of the city in the Book of Joshua. Then, God gave me the exact chapter and verse to find the city's name. When I found the verse, I was shocked to see the names of three towns; the middle one being where God would lead us. But I will not share the exact name in this book to protect the identities of those we met. Instead, I will refer to the town as "Buatan."

I looked for the name of Buatan on the map but couldn't find it. God spoke again, "Mark, you will not find the city on the map. I will lead you there."

Once we arrived in Malaysia, a missionary friend, who served in Malaysia, had prearranged for us to meet two young men, former Muslims. To protect their identity, I will not share their real names. I will refer to them as Ahmed and Jaffar.

We asked Ahmed and Jaffar if they would be our interpreters and go with us to Kelantan. "No, we might be killed evangelizing Muslims in Kelantan," they replied emphatically. "Furthermore, you are in our country, and it's our people you want to evangelize. We know them; they will attack you if you preach about Jesus," they continued.

However, wanting to appease us, they said, "We will go with you to Sabah, a safer place to share the gospel." I retorted, "God said He would perform miracles in Kelantan. We must believe and obey Him, no matter the risks. Jonah heaped trouble upon himself when he didn't obey God by not going to Nineveh, a dangerous city. I don't want to be like Jonah."

Ahmed and Jaffar inquired, "What methods do you use for evangelism?" We will demonstrate by example. I want to buy some local dresses for Kathy. Take us to a dress shop, and let's see what God does," I replied.

Once we arrived at the dress shop, straightaway, Kathy prophesized over the shop's owner, a Buddhist woman. Kathy's words, along with God's presence, whose glory rests on us, overwhelmed the owner. Encouraged by Kathy's ministry and compassion, the owner allowed us to minister to all her workers, a Buddhist seamstress, and three Muslim salesclerks.

The seamstress wanted prayer for severe pain in her hands, making it difficult to sew. She also suffered from debilitating depression. Kathy laid her hands on the seamstress and prayed as everyone in the shop curiously watched. Healing power flowed through Kathy's touch, and the seamstress was immediately set free from all her pain. Just as glorious, the Holy Spirit poured upon the seamstress the "oil of joy!" It was a beautiful sight to see her transform from gloom to glee. Her smile stretched from ear to ear as tears ran down her face. That miracle astounded all present and opened their hearts to hear and accept the Gospel with sincerity.

God gave me a word of knowledge over one of the Muslim salesclerks. Compassionately, I told her all about her abusive husband and the horrible things he did to her. The other salesclerks were frightened by the accuracy of my words. One of them said to their distressed friend, "How do you know this man? How does he know all these things about you?" "I never met this man before. I don't know how he knows these things," she replied with amazement and tears.

I went on to share that our God sees everything and that He not only loves them but deeply cares for them and desires to have an intimate relationship with them. I told the troubled salesclerk that Jesus wanted to help her on her journey through life. I shared the Gospel of salvation and testimonies of how Jesus has helped me through many trials and troubles. God granted them faith to believe, and all in that dress shop surrendered their lives to Jesus. Ahmed and Jaffar gave them Bibles and told them they would stay in touch.

God proved to Ahmed and Jaffar that the Holy Spirit powerfully moved through us. Encouraged by the dress shop experience, Ahmed and Jaffar enthusiastically agreed to travel to Kelantan with us. Then they melted our hearts with an endearing question. They inquired, "If you guys move to Malaysia, would you be our mom and dad." "Yes, and you can live with us, and we will teach you how to "fully" bring the Gospel of salvation to your people," we replied with big smiles.

Ahmed and Jaffar found Jesus supernaturally. Since it is forbidden for Muslims in Malaysia to convert to Christianity, finding someone willing to disciple them in God's Word was challenging. Also, they were eager to share their new faith with Muslims and did so with limited knowledge.

Ahmed and Jaffar's method were to leave tracts in public places and then depart quickly so as not to be incriminated. When we moved to Malaysia, we promised to teach them how to evangelize as done in the Book of Acts, which already began in the dress shop and continued in Kelantan.

When our friends from America arrived the next day, we all flew up to Kota Bharu, the capital of Kelantan. Upon arrival, we noticed billboards everywhere declaring Kota Bharu to be the Islamic Capital of S.E. Asia. That was no coincidence. God led us there at that specific time to proclaim that Jesus is the "King" of Kota Bharu.

The Holy Spirit prompted me to conduct several prophetic acts before engaging in evangelism. These unusual acts made no human sense, but I knew our obedience would release God's glory into the region, empowering our efforts and bringing success. That proved to be correct; many miraculous events and salvations followed. Blowing horns for seven days around Jericho didn't conform to human understanding. Yet, God's Spirit moved powerfully through their prophetic act.

After conducting several prophetic acts, we inquired with the locals if they knew of a village called Buatan. Repeatedly, their reply was no. Nevertheless, I trusted God would lead us to Buatan supernaturally; I knew I heard from God, and He was guiding us.

One morning, we stopped at a restaurant for breakfast. After eating, I went to pay our server, Iman. After introductions, I said to him, "We are Christians, and our God sent us to Malaysia to reveal His love for Muslims. One way our God reveals His love is through our prayers. Our God loves you, and He wants to bless you today. How could I ask my God to bless you?" Iman stood motionless and did not respond.

Seeing deep pain in his eyes, I continued, "We all have trouble, but I sense your trouble is crushing you. Would you tell me what's going on?" Iman sensed I genuinely loved and cared for him. With a quivering voice, he replied, "My mom has been terribly ill for twelve years, and my family and I have lost all hope for her healing. Would you pray for your God to heal my mother?" It was evident that Iman deeply loved his mother.

Iman knew my motive was not to convert him or prove Christianity was the true religion. To Imam, this encounter was about a white man believing that his God was able and willing to heal his mother. Iman gave me no specifics about his mother's condition; he only said his father had tried everything to find healing. I had faith this was a divine moment. I knew God would pour out His glory on Iman's family.

I shared with Iman the Bible story about a woman who suffered from an incurable blood disorder for twelve years. And that her community ostracized her because of her illness. Consequently, shame and disgrace became her constant companions.

Then I shared how God healed her when she touched the hem of Jesus' garment. And just as magnificent, how Jesus restored her dignity. I told Iman Jesus would do the same for his mother. This biblical story mesmerized Iman. I sensed he hoped Jesus would do the same for his mother. That was an extraordinary moment I will never forget; God gave faith to Iman to believe my testimonies.

Seeing Iman's faith, I offered, "Iman, we will gladly go to your parent's village and pray for your mother. Jesus will heal your mother, and you will see how much He loves you and your family. What is the name of the village where your mom and dad live?"

"My parents live in Buatan," he responded. My team and I were stunned. That was the prophetic word God gave me on the airplane; that He would do miracles in Buatan. My faith soared, and so did my team's confidence in my leadership. Iman told us the names of his parents—Abdullah and Mariah. He then gave us some vague directions to Buatan, and we swiftly took off. After two hours of driving through a highly forested region and many small villages, I asked Jaffar if he knew where he was going. He replied, "Dad, I am being led by Holy Spirit as you taught me." With skepticism, I said to Jaffar, "A man is walking on the road ahead of us. Let's stop and ask him if he knows the location of Buatan."

We parked our car in front of a dilapidated house that was next to the village mosque. Jaffar inquired of the man walking, "Do you know where Buatan is at?" "You are in Buatan," he answered. Amazed, we asked him, "Do you know a married couple, Abdullah and Mariah?" The man chuckled and replied, "You parked your vehicle right in front of their house." Later, we discovered that Iman's father was the village Imam (Muslim priest).

These miraculous signs compelled our faith to soar even higher; we were confident God was going to perform a mighty miracle in Buatan. Without a shadow of a doubt, we knew God was going to touch Iman's family with His miraculous love.

Buatan was a remote jungle village, and I'm sure the residents had never seen white people before. After introductions, Abdullah invited us into his house. We all sat down, and not leaving out any details, I shared how Jesus had brought us a long distance from America to Buatan to pray for Mariah. Abdullah, Mariah, their many children, and some neighbors were present. We had everyone's undivided attention, and it appeared to be going well until Mariah started manifesting demons.

Mariah suddenly arose and attacked Kathy and one of our friends. It was apparent she was possessed by evil spirits. Kathy and I had delivered several people from demon possession in America, so we were accustomed to demon manifestation and confident that Mariah would be set free.

In the Name of Jesus, I commanded the evil spirits to leave Mariah. They did not comply.

I asked Jesus, "What would you have us do?" Jesus answered, "Mariah opened a door for the demons to enter. Ask Abdullah what happened to Mariah, and he will reveal that door, then close it. But first, bind the demons from manifesting. After you have closed the door, cast out the demons."

Trusting Jesus, I looked into Mariah's eyes and said, "In the name of Jesus, I command you evil spirits to stop manifesting." Instantly, Mariah's eyes turned inside out, and she crashed to the floor, falling backward. Everyone in the room was stunned and terrified.

With Jaffar interpreting, I asked Abdullah how his wife became demonized. I told him that if he cooperated with me, Jesus would set his wife free. Shocked and encouraged by my authority over demons, Abdullah complied to follow my guidance. Abdullah knew this was not a religious attempt to convert him but a spiritual encounter with mysterious powers that might set his wife free from demonic possession. Abdullah, an Imam, became submissive to all my instructions and listened intently to what I said about Jesus!

Abdullah shared that Mariah had an affair with a neighbor. But after some time, she broke off the relationship hoping to restore their marriage. However, enraged over the breakup, the neighbor paid a witch doctor to bury an accursed object in their backyard. The witch doctor then cast a spell on Mariah. Abdullah said for the last twelve years, Mariah acted insanely.

Often, she would strip naked and run around the village attacking and cursing anyone in her sight.

I reassured Abdullah that Jesus sent us to Buatan for the very purpose of setting Mariah free from demonic possession and healing her of her inflictions.

Then, I asked Jesus, "What would you have me do now?" Following Jesus' instructions, I got a shovel and, along with a friend, went out to the backyard to dig up the accursed object. The practice of witchcraft in Malaysia dates before the arrival of Islam. Pagan rituals and casting spells have been part of the Malaysian culture for thousands of years. Furthermore, most Malaysians are terrified when they know a witch doctor has released a curse on them.

I shared a scripture from Deuteronomy 7:25-26. In that scripture, God warns us that bringing an accursed object into our house will bring destruction. I also shared when we confess and repent of our sins, in Jesus' Name, we can break off all curses. Everyone in the room listened intently.

While I dug up the accursed object, my team prayed over Mariah as she lay on the floor in a comatose state. About two hours later, I finally dug up the demonic item and shouted, "In the Mighty Name of Jesus, I break the power that's behind this accursed object." My pronouncement agitated the demons possessing Mariah. Swiftly, she sprung from the floor and started trashing the place.

I ran into the house, looked into Mariah's eyes, and commanded the demons to be silent in the Name of Jesus. Also, I commanded the evil spirits not to cause Mariah to go into another demonic coma. The demons obeyed. I then asked Mariah to sit down on a chair, and she complied.

Sensing more needed to be done before I cast out the demons, I asked Jesus, "What would you have me do now?" Jesus replied, "Mariah believes she is forever condemned for her adultery and betrayal. Guilt, shame, and self-condemnation have imprisoned her. However, Abdullah has the keys to set her free. Instruct Abdullah to perform a prophetic act. Tell him to get a washbasin, fill it with water, and wash Mariah's feet as a symbolic act that God is cleansing her from her sin. Tell Abdullah as he washes his wife's feet to look into her eyes, and with sincerity, say, 'I forgive you, please forgive yourself.'"

Abdullah did everything I instructed. With tears streaming down his cheeks, he looked into his wife's eyes, and with a trembling voice, said, "I have forgiven you; please forgive yourself." We all carefully observed to see what might happen. You could hear a pin drop in the house. Forgiveness was the key to releasing her from her prison. If she forgave herself, she would be set free. The demons used guilt, shame, and self-condemnation as an opportunity to possess and torment Mariah. Looking into Mariah's eyes, I sensed she accepted her husband's loving forgiveness. I also perceived Mariah forgave herself; her countenance had shifted from despair to hope. Then I received a strong prompting to cast out the demons.

With an authoritative voice, and in the Name of Jesus, I commanded all the demons to leave Mariah. Like water erupting from a broken pipe, suddenly, Mariah opened her mouth, and vomit shot out everywhere. Everyone present was astounded. It was evident to Mariah's family and neighbors she was free. Kathy then prayed, and God healed Mariah of her illnesses. We made sure Jesus got all the glory for Mariah's deliverance and healing.

Jubilation washed away all gloom. Abdullah got his wife back, and all the children got their mother back. No words can express the joy of the moment.

Then, astoundingly, Abdullah said, "I prayed to Allah for twelve years to save my wife, and I never heard a whisper from him. I want a Bible, and I want to learn about Jesus. Today, I have seen power from Jesus and His love for us." We gave Abdullah a Bible and told him we would visit them often. I shared the gospel of salvation with all present, and that salvation was a gift. Wonderfully, the entire family followed my guidance. They confessed and repented of their sins and became Christ's disciples. I reassured everyone their sins were permanently washed away by the precious Blood of Jesus! Muslims believe they have no Savior and must pay the penalty of their sins. So our message of salvation was Good News!

Boundless elation broke out, and all present glorified Jesus. Twelve years of torment, depression, and despair vanished in a moment as heaven invaded their home. Jaffar instructed all the children to sit in a circle on the floor. He then taught them a beautiful Christian song in their language. They all sang with inexpressible joy!

God performed many other miracles on this exploratory mission trip. Hence, God convincingly confirmed our "calling"! We now had the confidence to sell all our possessions, leave our home and family, and move to Malaysia. God removed all our insecurities and strengthened our faith.

The Christian religion is very peculiar and many times offensive to most who follow other faiths. Only by God's grace will they believe the Gospel of Salvation. Miraculous signs and wonders accompanying our message of grace have always been part of God's plans.

For when we brought you the Good News, it was not only with words but also with power, for the Holy Spirit gave you full assurance that what we said was true. And you know of our concern for you from the way we lived when we were with you (1 Thessalonians 1:5 NLT).

Reflections

Kathy and I were uncertain that God was calling us to be His servants and ambassadors to Malaysia. We both desired to go, but we knew it would not sit well with our family and friends. Moreover, with Kathy's mom suffering from an incurable disease and our children about to have children, it appeared foolish to go. Furthermore, strong opposition met us at every step.

Wonderfully, God was faithful to reassure us of our calling through this short-term mission trip. God confirmed our calling through miraculous signs and wonders and best of all, Muslims surrendering their lives to Jesus. Moreover, God gave us unusual peace that transcended all our insecurities. All our worries vanished. Without a shadow of a doubt, we knew God would take care of our family and be our "Defender" to those who doubted and opposed our calling.

If you are wrestling with doubt about God calling you for a specific purpose or not, don't lose heart. Beseech God for confirmation and guidance. God not only loves you, but He also deeply cares for you. If you seek God with a sincere heart, He will not hesitate to overshadow you with His loving grace and peace as He clarifies His plans and purposes. You will never be ashamed for trusting Jesus for guidance. Instead, He will empower your faith to soar and give you divine confidence that He is guiding your steps. Moreover, you will find that His plans are far greater than anything you could imagine (see 1 Corinthians 2:9).

God Speaks Through a Cow

Prompted by the Holy Spirit, we embarked on an evangelical outreach in Kelantan, a northern Malaysian State, which shares a border with Thailand. We had no specific destination in mind, but trusted God would be our Guide. We started our days in prayer and worship, knowing we could accomplish nothing outside God's grace. In those precious times, God always gave us a fresh anointing of peace and confidence to face any uncertain circumstances we might encounter.

Kelantan is a hard-core Islamic region that strongly opposes Christianity with laws that prohibit evangelizing Muslims. For those found guilty of doing so, their penalty is caning and a two-year prison sentence. Nevertheless, God's love and plans for salvation for the lost have no boundaries.

As we drove on a road that meandered through jungle villages, we suddenly approached a large cow lying in the middle of the road, making it impossible to pass. We sensed God caused that cow to lay down on the road for a purpose, so we sought His guidance in prayer.

A friend of ours who had joined us on this mission trip, who is a Vietnam Vet, stated, "This terrain reminds me of Vietnam. I sense I have unfinished business, and it might be somewhere here." That was an understatement. God had prearranged an unexpected visit with a Muslim family living just off the main road from where the cow was lying. God wanted to bring salvation and healing to this family and inner healing to our veteran friend.

Directly from where our vehicle stalled, a muddy path led to a house about 100 yards away. We felt God wanted us to share the Gospel with the family who lived there. So, we drove our old rickety rental van down a muddy path and parked in front of a dilapidated house.

13

An elderly man, Zaman, warmly greeted us and invited us to sit with him and his family in a shady area for drinks and snacks. He was married with many children, and all were present. Though they were impoverished, their culture honors strangers as family.

Zaman asked what our purpose was for visiting Malaysia. Overwhelmed with compassion for this family, I shared the Gospel of Salvation and what it cost God to forgive us of all our sins, including the most wicked! I emphasized that salvation only comes by God's grace and through the forgiveness of sins. I accentuated Jesus and the meaning of His crucifixion!

I stressed how much Heavenly Father loved Zaman and his family. And, as I always do, I shared my personal testimony of how God brought me from a horrendous life of sin to a place of joy, peace, and righteousness. Zaman and his family patiently and intently listened.

We then asked Zaman to share about his life. Zaman sadly shared that he and his family escaped death by fleeing Cambodia and relocating to Malaysia. The Khmer Rouge regime (the communist party of Kampuchea) viciously massacred more than one million Hmong from 1975 to 1979. When the Americans pulled their military from Vietnam and the surrounding countries, the Khmer Rouge regime cruelly killed all those deemed supporters of America. Zaman told us that all their family and relatives were dead; they were the only ones to escape.

Deep sorrow overcame us as we heard this broken man speak about how his relatives and friends were brutally murdered because of the American pullout. What made it worse, the American government knew that would happen but ordered the evacuation, nevertheless. The Hmong volunteered to help the American military in the Vietnam war, so they felt tremendously betrayed.

Tears ran down our faces as Zaman continued to share his pain and suffering. Overcome with guilt and shame, our Vietnam Vet friend wept and asked for Zaman's forgiveness. "My American patriots and I have done a horrible crime to you and your people. On behalf of all Americans, would you forgive us for abandoning you and your people, he asked?" It was a very delicate and surreal moment. Everyone's emotions were raw and sensitive.

Convicted by the testimony of Jesus and our friend's confession, Zaman humbly stated, "I believe your words about Jesus to be true. I see that it cost God a great price to forgive us of our sins. And I believe God did so because He loves us. I must be like-minded, so I forgive you and America." Zaman spoke with sincerity and honor. Rarely have I witnessed this type of humility. Our mission work is full of hardships, struggles, and persecution. Our reward is seeing God's grace come upon His lost children bringing them to salvation. Those precious moments bring meaning to our sufferings and encouragement to press on!

Zaman chose to forgive the atrocious sins against him, his family, and his country. Zaman believed the "Good News" and surrendered his life to Jesus. Consequently, God poured out His grace, healing Zaman of bitterness and the darkness it brought. It was a glorious sight to witness Zaman's newfound joy and peace.

"Blessed are the merciful, for they shall receive mercy!" Matthew 5:7

It's an extraordinary event when a person receives God's Spirit and eternal life. This humble man's countenance quickly went from despair to inexpressible joy. Zaman was a man filled with hatred towards Americans, but Jesus swiftly released him from imprisonment to bitterness.

Over the next several months, we visited this family several times. It brought us great delight to see them rejoicing in their new faith. However, sadly, their neighbors informed the local Islamic religious police that a white married couple was evangelizing in the region.

Zaman called and told us that the police planned to detain and imprison us. Moreover, he stated the police had instructed all their neighbors to report us if we returned to their city. Zaman wept and told us not to come back to their place.

This scenario frequently happened to us in our evangelical endeavors. Nevertheless, we know we planted seeds of eternal life in many hearts! We gave Bibles to all those we led to Jesus. Some have secretly informed us they hide their Bibles because they cherish them.

I will never judge others as they endure threats of persecution. This family had experienced the worst horrors of life and were reluctant to go through more. In Cambodia, they were of the Buddhist faith, but the Malaysian government forced them to convert to Islam. If they didn't accept Islam as their faith, the Malaysian authorities would send them back to Cambodia, where they would undoubtedly suffer a horrible death. We continue to pray God gives them the grace to grow in their new faith and that Holy Spirit guides them. Also, we pray that God perfects His love in their hearts because perfect love casts out all fear (see 1 John 4:18).

The religious police want to detain us in many Muslim communities. However, we ignore those threats and return to those who desire to grow in Jesus' teachings. Many of our converts love Jesus and us more than they fear persecution. We continue to visit them despite threats of persecution.

Throughout history, many saints have been jailed and killed for the Gospel. Though we hope that isn't our fate, we desire to be like-minded and honor God's will more than our lives.

A cow lying on the road prevented us from proceeding. We asked God, "What would you have us do?" That was an excellent question to ask.

"Don't be afraid of those who want to kill your body; they cannot touch your soul. Fear only God, who can destroy both soul and body in hell" (Matthew 10:28 NLT).

Reflections

God often gets our attention through unusual events. In these bizarre moments, if we seek God for revelation, He is faithful to provide us with wisdom and guidance. We could have been annoyed by the cow's refusal to move. But, knowing God is in all the details of our lives, we sought Him for understanding rather than honking our horn until the cow got up and left.

God loves ALL people, and He led us to this Cambodian family to deliver them from the kingdom of darkness to the kingdom of light. Hearing and obeying God's voice through the cow lying on the road brought this humble and precious family healing, restoration, redemption, and salvation. It also brought inner healing to our friend. ALL of Heaven celebrated that day, and Jesus received another reward for His suffering.

Things don't always appear as they seem. Ask God to give you grace so that you can be sensitive to the many ways He speaks. Don't worry about making mistakes; Jesus is the Lord of your entire life, including your missteps. Jesus is gentle, patient, and humble. With His loving kindness, Jesus will help you grow in hearing His voice if you are willing to grow. Moreover, God will use you for His mighty purposes if you remain committed to expressing your faith through love.

Revival Comes to a Muslim City
Amid an "Islamic uprising"

⟨∞∞⟩

While we lived in Malaysia, there was an Islamic uprising against the local Christians over Allah's name. In the heat of their anger, some Muslims burned a few churches. Consequently, fear swept through the Christian community. Muslim radicals had murdered many Christians during an earlier uprising, so their worry was understandable.

During the religious unrest, I asked Jesus, "What would you have us do?" Jesus replied, "Go to Kota Bharu and conduct a revival service in the Central Marketplace—next to the large Mosque." Wow! His assignment appeared impossible. Jesus instructed us to preach His Gospel of Salvation to Muslims during an Islamic uprising. "Was Jesus asking us to be martyred," we wondered? It didn't matter; the Holy Spirit gave us a burning desire to go. Throughout history, God has moved most powerfully through those who did not surrender to fear because of dangerous circumstances but instead trusted and obeyed God. This was an opportunity for us to honor God with radical obedience.

We knew we could not accomplish this assignment without God going with us. All our talents, skills, and giftings would be meaningless without God's presence. Gratefully, after much prayer God gave us peace. We knew God would use our vessels powerfully to reveal His glory.

Kota Bharu is the capital of Kelantan, a Malaysian State bordering Thailand. We had traveled to Kota Bharu in 2005 when they declared their city to be the Islamic Capital of Southeast Asia. While we stayed in Kota Bharu, Holy Spirit instructed us to perform some prophetic acts and proclaim Jesus, King of Kota Bharu. We believed those prophetic acts and declarations released God's glory and angels into the region. Thus, they prepared a spiritual climate to boldly preach the Good News accompanied by miracles.

On the surface, going to Kota Bharu during this unrest appeared suicidal. Nevertheless, Kathy and I don't take risks assessments when God tells us to go; we obey God and go! Frequently, well-intentioned friends warn us to be wise and not foolish before embarking on evangelical outreaches. Basically, they are asking us to take a risk assessment. If we believe God has spoken, that type of wisdom is second-guessing.

That corruptible reasoning did not bode well for the Israelites fleeing captivity in Egypt. They did not believe in God's promise of success. Instead, they succumbed to fear by allowing human reasoning to have a greater voice than God's. They looked at all the dangerous circumstances and determined it was impossible to conquer the land God promised. Subsequently, fear overcame them, choking out all their faith. And without faith, God could not use them to fulfill His purposes.

Consequently, the Israelites did not inherit the "promised land." Only by faith do we receive God's promises. To me, wisdom is to get on my knees and cry out, "Lord, what would you have us do?" And then do it. As I mentioned, the most significant moments in history came when God's children didn't allow fear a place of influence in their souls. But, instead, they trusted God and refused to yield imminent danger. We understand we don't always hear correctly from God. It does not matter; we believe that if our motives are pure and we earnestly desire to express our faith through compassion, God will be with us and bless our efforts.

Kathy believed me when I said God wanted us to conduct a revival meeting in Kota Bharu. Not succumbing to fear, Kathy was excited and expectant God would do something miraculous on this evangelical outreach. God gave me the most wonderful wife and partner.

When we arrived in Kota Bharu, we decided to walk through the marketplace and wait for God's instructions. Many merchants were displaying their goods on tables throughout the area. Being the only white people, we stuck out like blinking neon signs—all eyes were on us. In the middle of the marketplace, I asked our Lord, "Now that we have arrived, what would you have us do." The Holy Spirit prompted me to pray a blessing over a woman merchant (Mariah) who appeared depressed.

After introductions, I gently declared to Mariah, "We are Christians, and our God sent us to Kota Bharu to bless those we meet. Our God loves Muslims, and so do we." I then described the character of our God: kind, gentle, patient, loving, and full of mercy. I told her it brought our God great joy to bless people. I then asked her if I could pray and ask my God to bless her. She did not hesitate and eagerly asked for her business to be blessed. She lamented that she had no customers that day. I put my faith on the line and responded, "My God will answer your prayer request and bring customers to you immediately. However, when they come, you must thank and praise Jesus only because I am praying in His name and not in the name of any other god." She understandably complied.

God swiftly answered my prayer, and customers came to her table straightaway. The woman merchant was stunned and openly praised and thanked Jesus for His goodness. That encounter opened the door for revival in the marketplace that day.

Another Muslim lady, who watched God answer my prayer, approached me and said, "Sir, can you pray for me to be healed? I have much pain in my body." Her countenance spoke loudly of her despair. I told her my wife would pray for her. It was evident God had granted us unusual favor in the most incomprehensible circumstances.

A curious crowd gathered to observe Kathy praying for the sick woman. Kathy instructed the lady to sit down on a brick bench to put her at ease. The woman pointed to her shoulder, showing Kathy where her pain was. Not be disturbed by the precarious surroundings, Kathy closed her eyes, placed her hand on the woman's shoulder, and prayed. After a few moments, Kathy asked the woman if she felt better. "No, I am the same," the woman replied sadly. Kathy continued to pray and periodically stopped several more times to inquire if she felt better. Each time the woman would reply, "No, the pain is the same."

Kathy is a most remarkable person. She is tenacious and relentless when it comes to prayer; she will not give up. At the same time, Kathy was praying, I was sharing the Gospel with the crowd. However, I kept a continuous eye on Kathy.

Kathy's faith appeared to hit the ceiling; she was struggling. Then the most amazing thing happened. Kathy looked up to Heaven and set her eyes on Jesus. Jesus responded by bringing Kathy to a new horizon of faith. With fresh inspiration, Kathy engaged in pray with greater intensity. Curiously, the crowd patiently watched. Suddenly, the sick woman looked into Kathy's eyes and gleefully expressed, "The pain in my shoulder is gone. Please pray for my hip." Jesus healed her hip quickly, then she wanted prayer for her knee, then her feet. Jesus gave this marketplace woman a complete overhaul; many Muslims observed with awe and wonder. That miraculous healing encouraged several other marketplace women to seek Kathy for healing prayer. God's glory pierced through the darkness and invaded the hearts of many staunch Muslims that glorious day.

While Kathy was praying for the women, I was preaching a blasphemous message to the crowd!According to the Islamic faith, God does not have a son; claiming so is sacrilegious and contemptuous of their religious laws. However, it was apparent by the crowd's demeanor that God had opened their ears and hearts to hear and ponder His Word and my testimonies.

To explain Jesus as God's only begotten Son, I told the crowd that Jesus has no beginning or end; He is eternal, same as His Father. I emphasized that Jesus was not created and willingly took the form of a human to bring us salvation. I taught Jesus is the exact representation of His Father in Heaven. I explained why Jesus had to leave His heavenly place and come to earth. I preached the reason for Christ's crucifixion and His plan for salvation. At the same time, I was wrestling with evil spirits.

It never left my mind that our activity was illegal, and things could go badly, quickly. We were promoting Christianity to a group of staunch Muslims amid heightened religious unrest. Nevertheless, it was apparent that the Holy Spirit was powerfully convicting their hearts. Moreover, God was confirming my message with miraculous healings.

At the time, we were not proficient in the Malay language, so we asked a Malaysian Christian friend to accompany us on this mission trip. He is a wonderful young man who passionately loves Jesus. After about twenty minutes of sharing the gospel with the crowd, my friend turned to me and said, "Mark, you better stop speaking. The men look very angry and could attack us at any moment. Your message is upsetting them." I replied, "Yes, they look angry, but let me ask Heavenly Father, why?"

God spoke to me clearly, "Mark, they see Kathy blessing the marketplace women; they want prayer too! Go pray for them." I complied and asked the men if they would like prayer. They did. They told me they had been waiting for an invitation! Amazing! It didn't matter that we were Christians. They all knew they were experiencing something glorious that had never happened in their lives before, and they didn't want to be left out.

I inquired of the first man, "How can I pray for you?" "I have severe stomach pain," He replied. I told him that I would ask my God to reveal the source of the pain, and then I would pray. After hearing from God, I looked into the man's eyes and, with compassion, stated, "My God told me that you are an accountant and that your boss is forcing you to commit fraud. You are a man of integrity, and you feel guilty and shameful for participating in your bosses' scheme. Anxiety has caused you to have a painful ulcer. I will pray for the ulcer to disappear and the pain to go. That will be a sign my God hears my prayers and cares for you. Also, God has told me that you must go to your boss and tell him that you will no longer participate in his scam. And if you do this, my God will give you favor." The accountant was astounded by the accuracy of my words. Everything I said was true. He gratefully allowed me to pray.

After a short prayer, God set him free from all his pain. I prayed for several other Muslim men that day while Kathy was praying for many sick marketplace women. Right when everything seemed to be going well, things took a worrisome turn!

An elderly Muslim man of prominence walked into the marketplace. Later, I found out he was a retired, high-ranking police officer who still carried a lot of influence. As he approached me, everyone's faces went from joy to gloom. I knew what everyone was thinking, "The white couple is going to get arrested. The party is over." But God had other plans!

The retired policeman briskly came to me and in English and with authority asked, "What are you doing in the marketplace?" "My God sent us to Kota Bharu to pray for the sick and hurting," I responded. I then asked him, "Sir, do you have any pain in your body? If you are willing, I will pray for my God to heal you." All eyes were on our conversation. He replied, "Arthritis has caused terrible pain in my right knee for two years. Yes, you can pray for me." I asked him to sit on a bench, which he did. Then the devil attempted to exploit one of my weaknesses to shame me and pervert God's will.

Our spiritual sons, former Muslims, told me never to emit gas in the presence of Muslims. Muslims in Malaysia believe that when someone flatulates, that is a sign demons are being discharged from their behind. What happened next was embarrassing, but it's an essential part of this story, so I must share it. Curry is a popular ingredient in Malaysian food dishes, and curry gave me lots of gas. Unfortunately, my discharges were unpredictable and difficult to restrain.

As I bent over to lay my hand on the retired policeman's knee, I accidentally erupted. It was loud. Instantly, distressing thoughts flooded my mind—from the devil, of course. I thought, "Everyone watching heard my eruption and believed I just discharged demons from my behind. God would certainly not answer my prayer after that." Gratefully, Holy Spirit reminded me that He is greater than any unexpected ghastly occurrences and always in control. I have learned to place my faith only in one truth, "God is good all the time." I never set my confidence in my character, skin color, education, training, or giftings, only in Jesus!

After placing my hand on the man's knee, I silently prayed, "Jesus, if you would like Kathy and me to serve you another day, I think it would be best if you healed this man." My prayer was not impressive, but it was from my heart. God was pleased with my faith and healed the retired policeman. The former policeman was in awe of being miraculously healed. With much gratitude, he bought us supper in the marketplace to show us his appreciation. Humorously, we were served more curry. However, Jesus delivered me from that condition after prayer. Thank goodness!!

The testimonies of that day quickly spread throughout the region. That was both good and bad. Encouraged by the reports, many Muslims with pure hearts and honest motives sought to hear more about our faith and receive prayer. Others, which included police officers, conspired to have us murdered. However, God was faithful to hide us in His light. We frequently received a forewarning of an impending ambush, allowing us to make alternate plans. Other times, we seemed to mysteriously evade and hide from those pursuing us.

When some radical Muslims burned Christian churches, we asked God, "What would you have us do?" Our obedience led to a revival in the least likely place and God was glorified!

Proclaim the Word of God and stand upon it no matter what! Rise to the occasion and preach when it is convenient and when it is not. Preach in the full expression of the Holy Spirit —with wisdom and patience as you instruct and teach the people (2 Timothy 4:2—TPT).

Reflections

The Ninevites caused indescribable violence, torture, and death to the Israelites. They are some of the most violent and murderous people in history. Jonah and the Israelites hoped they would experience God's fiery judgment. However, God desired to demonstrate the depths of His mercy by sending Jonah to be His representative. Jonah hated and despised the Ninevites and did not want to fulfill God's plans. Nevertheless, he relented and declared God's warning to them. The Ninevites repented from their evil ways and turned to God.

Similarly, the majority of Christian Malaysians detested the Malay Muslims. They had experienced many generations of inequalities and suffering from their Muslim countrymen and hoped for their demise. However, God sent us to declare His Word and reveal His mercy to the Muslims amid the Islamic uprising. Beautifully, many repented and turned to Jesus for healing and salvation.

There may be someone in your family or workplace that is causing you much suffering. God might be calling you to be His voice of mercy (see Luke 6:27-28). Always remember, mercy is greater than judgment (see James 2:13). God does not want anyone to perish but for all to repent (see 2 Peter 3:9). God might be asking you to bring salvation to someone who has hurt you. If so, and you obey, God will bless you with incredible joy (see Matthew 5:7 & 11).

A Prophetic Word Saves a Muslim Girl from Suicide

Nearly 230,000 precious lives died from the 2004 Indian ocean earthquake and tsunami. Millions of other lives were tragically impacted. Kuala Muda, Malaysia, was not spared; tens of thousands perished in this region, as well.

Two of our spiritual sons, Jaffar and Ahmed, former Muslims, had ministered in Kuala Muda and wanted us to meet some of the residents. Our sons were eager to have us share the Good News with them. They had shown the community benevolence but not shared the gospel of salvation.

Kuala Muda is mostly a farming region with rice paddies covering the landscape in all directions. As we drove down narrow, muddy roads, no workers could be seen in the fields. The tsunami had contaminated the region with salt, and it would take five years for the rains to restore the fields. Until then, planting seeds would be a pointless effort and a waste of valuable resources.

Kuala Muda was destitute, and its people were hopelessly lost in despair. The death of family and friends, destruction of houses and fishing boats, and fields that yielded no crops embraced their suffering. Our hearts ached over their plight. However, godly mourning always compels us to bring compassion, relief, and hope to those grieving.

Jesus is the answer when tragedy strikes. For those who put their faith in Jesus, He will bring joy for mourning and beauty from ashes. We were excited to share Jesus and His Gospel with the residents. Also, we were eager to help them in their desperation. We brought with us lots of food and other essential items.

26

The kingdom of God is within us, and Jesus is our King. He mends broken hearts, heals the sick, restores families, and redeems what's lost. Jesus is a Miracle Worker. Our mission was obvious to reveal Jesus and His Kingdom to Kuala Muda.

On an earlier trip to Kuala Muda, Jaffar told several farmers Jesus was going to do a miracle in their midst. They did not have a complete understanding of biblical Jesus, but they were open to a miracle in their despair.

Jaffar gathered some farmers and their families around a barren field and prayed for Heavenly Father to heal their land in the Name of Jesus. After praying, Jaffar gave the farmers money and encouraged them to buy and plant rice seeds by faith. They complied, and miraculously, rice sprung forth from the soil at its appropriate time. That miracle spread throughout the community and opened the hearts of many Muslims to Jesus and His Gospel. Jaffar and Ahmed wanted us to meet a particular Muslim family they loved.

However, they could not remember precisely where they lived. We slowly drove through an area with many tiny square cement houses that looked the same. Seeing a house that appeared familiar, Jaffar said, "I think this is the place; let's stop here. I think this is their house."

The front door was open, so Jaffar shouted, "Hello, is anyone home." A shirtless man wearing only tattered shorts and flip flops from the back of the house marched our way. He appeared very angry. Jaffar anxiously said, "Dad, this is the wrong house; I don't know that man; he looks like a Taliban; let's get out of here quickly." "Yes, he looks angry, but let's see why. Let me direct the conversation; you translate," I replied. Jaffar nervously agreed. After introductions, straightaway, I asked the man why he appeared so angry.

Ragefully, he stated that the Malaysian government had provided tsunami relief for everyone in the community except him and his family. He said he had filled out all the required forms, but the government officials kept stonewalling him.

God always gives me unique wisdom when presenting the Good News in precarious situations. This time was no exception. The man listened carefully and was encouraged by my words, bringing him a measure of hope.

I encouraged this desperate man to put his faith in Jesus for a miracle. I told him Jesus was real and not only loved him but deeply cared for him. He graciously agreed to repeat after me in prayer. We prayed, "Jesus, if you are the Son of God who came to save the world, please give me favor with the Malaysian government so that I can get my relief support." I then told him to go to the government office and refile for tsunami aid as soon as possible. Before we departed, we prayed a blessing over him.

There is no doubt the Holy Spirit inspired my words. No matter how scary or inconvenient, every situation is an opportunity to plant kingdom seeds. Our unplanned visit brought hope and peace to this distraught and angry man. With sincerity, he thanked us for our prayers. He had no phone, so there was no way of following up.

Moreover, we have countless unexpected similar encounters, and there is no way we could conceivably follow up on all of them. Some plant, some water, and others harvest. We planted powerful kingdom seeds into that man's heart. All Christians have bushels of kingdom seed within them. Only when we arrive in Heaven will we fully see the fruit of our efforts. We got into our car and continued down the same rickety road. Finally, Jaffar recognized the intended house. They had no phone either, so this Muslim family had no forewarning that we were coming.

As we walked up to the front door, my heart raced with expectation. In my spirit, I sensed this family was going to have an amazing encounter with God. The family warmly greeted us and asked us to come in. After introductions, we all sat on the floor. Culturally, most Malaysians living in the villages prefer to sit on the floor instead of furniture. Many cannot afford furniture.

Once seated and after some casual conversation, the Holy Spirit compelled Kathy to share a prophetic word for the family's mother, Aatifa. The entire family was overcome by the accuracy of Kathy's prophecy, and even more so, her compassion. God has blessed Kathy with the gift of prophecy, and she has learned to use it eloquently in her evangelism efforts. Kathy also has a powerful healing gift that has opened the eyes of multitudes to see and experience God's kindness and mercy.

As I shared the Good News with this precious family, I felt compelled to emphasize Heavenly Father's forgiveness of sins through the sacrifice of His only begotten Son. The family was captivated when I stated that God's grace was for everyone, including Muslims. And that anyone could experience abundant life despite their sin, persecution, trials, or troubles.

When I have the honor to share God's love and plan for salvation with the lost and hurting, it is when I feel the closest to God; they are precious moments that I will forever cherish in my heart. I had no idea at the time that my message would forever change the direction of this humble family.

Shortly later, while we were all chatting, my eyes were drawn to their 15-year-old daughter, Amira. Holy Spirit spoke to me, "Mark, recently she was horribly hurt and rejected. She has lost all hope for a happy life and is determined to commit suicide." At first, I wrestled with doubt, "Did I actually hear from God." Amira appeared to be happy. She remained engaged in our conversations with a cheerful demeanor. However, the prompting to share what God revealed to me became stronger and stronger; it became unbearable for me to remain silent.

So, with compassion and trepidation, I looked into Amira's eyes and stated, "Jesus, whom we have been talking about, has shared something with me about your life. Please forgive me if I have misheard, but I feel compelled to share what I believe Jesus shared with me. Recently, something horrible has happened to you that has caused you great suffering. Your pain is so deep you have lost all hope for happiness and, as a result, you have decided to take your life. In fact, you plan to do it this week. Jesus loves you and still has a purpose and plan to bless your life. If you believe in Jesus and trust Him, Jesus will heal and restore you and bring you into a season of peace and joy.

Immediately, Amira's countenance shifted to profound grief. She abruptly rose and ran out of the house, screaming. Her screams were louder than any I have ever heard; her torment pierced our hearts and caused us to cry out for God to reveal His mercy and healing. After 40 minutes of wailing, Amira came back into the house. She had calmed down. I believe our prayers brought her a measure of comfort. I asked Jesus, "What happened to Amira that caused this great anguish." Jesus replied, "I want to spare them from humiliation; you don't need to know."

Overcome by awe and fear, the entire family eagerly accepted Jesus as their Lord and Savior! God used all our giftings to bring salvation that day. Kathy's prophecy, my word of knowledge, our humanitarian aid, sharing the gospel of salvation, and the prayers of our Intercessors. All our giftings worked beautifully together to bring salvation to this humble family.

Everyone rejoiced in God's goodness and faithfulness. It did not matter that we didn't know Amira's circumstances; she had found hope in Jesus and was no longer suicidal.

A few months later, we revisited the family. They shared with us what led to Amira's desire to commit suicide. She had been raped and impregnated by a neighbor, which became a sticky dilemma for the family. In their culture, a woman who gets pregnant out of wedlock is labeled a whore and can be jailed. Even if the pregnancy was due to rape. Moreover, the baby is labeled a bastard and taken to an unbearable institution for orphans.

Though they loved their daughter dearly, her rape brought shame to the family. They were caught in an 'if we do or do not' predicament. Laws required them to report their daughter's unholy pregnancy to the authorities. Doing so could bring a tragic ending to their daughter's life. If they did not file a report, they could be prosecuted and punished. They were contemplating banishing their daughter from the family - and she knew it!

Nevertheless, God showed this precious family how much He cares for them. Consequently, they put their hope in Jesus and trusted Him for their fate. Miraculously, they were spared from governmental persecution.

On our second trip, we brought a Pastor (Ezekiel) who lived in a nearby city.

Ezekiel has a heart for Muslims to know Jesus, so we appointed and anointed him to take on the pastoral duties to disciple this precious family.

When we arrived, we were met with long hugs, lots of kisses, and broad smiles! Amira's father, Ahmed, was so delighted to have a pastor disciple them; he gave Ezekiel a very long body massage—with oil—to honor him.

With much gratitude, Ahmed expressed in his own words, "We were convicted by your message, prophetic words, acts of kindness, and compassionate prayers. Thank you for telling us about Jesus. We decided to forgive our neighbor and accept our new grandchild, as God accepts us!"

In the same way, there is more joy in heaven over one lost sinner who repents and returns to God than over ninety-nine others who are righteous and haven't strayed away (Luke 15:7—NLT)!

Reflections

God's Word instructs us to seek the gifts of the Holy Spirit. However, expressing God's love to others must be our highest goal when seeking spiritual gifts (see 1 Corinthians 14:1).

One of the gifts I have sought is "Words of Knowledge" (see 1 Corinthians 12:8). I was reluctant to share with Amira and her family what I thought God was sharing with me. I needed peace to do so. I did not want to, unintentionally, bring confusion and despair. God not only gave me peace but an extra measure of compassion. I learned that God will always bring peace when we seek Him with a sincere heart, no matter how dire our circumstances are.

My "Word of Knowledge" brought salvation to Amira and her family. I have used this precious gift to bless multitudes around the world. All glory to God!

The gifts of the Holy Spirit are for anyone who believes in Jesus (see John 14:12). Don't let a spirit of intimidation keep you from fanning into flames the gifts He has for you. Seek God for boldness and use your gifts to bring encouragement, correction, comfort, understanding, healing, or salvation to others (see 2 Timothy 2:6-7). Don't worry about making mistakes when using your gifts. If your highest motive is to love others, be assured God will fan your gifts into flames.

A Buddhist doctor surrenders his life to Jesus then dies!

Early in our ministry in Malaysia, two of our spiritual sons, Ahmed and Jaffar, pleaded with us to pray for a former neighbor, Uncle Chen, who was perilously ill. Uncle Chen was a retired doctor who followed Buddhism. They described Uncle Chen as a cranky old guy who hated Christianity. Supposedly, because he lived next to a church whose worship was loud and obnoxious, in his own mind!

Our sons stated that Uncle Chen's doctor gave him a death sentence, and he was ominously close to passing. We accepted the invitation to pray for Uncle Chen and immediately went to his house. Uncle Chen's wife greeted us warmly and led us into his bedroom, where he was lying on his bed waiting to die. Darkness impregnated the atmosphere with deep sorrow. Uncle Chen was sullen and drowning in despair. Our mission was to shine God's glory into the doom and gloom.

I have led multitudes who hated Christianity to a saving relationship with Jesus, so I had faith God would do the same for Uncle Chen. I asked Uncle Chen if I could share my testimony. With some reluctance, he complied. He was desperate for a miracle and open to anything.

I passionately shared how Jesus had miraculously healed me and others through my prayers. I also shared the Gospel of Salvation. Uncle Chen hung on every word I spoke; they appeared to bring him a measure of hope.

Seeing he had faith, I asked, "Uncle Chen, I could pray for Jesus to heal you. But you could have something much more splendid. You could obtain eternal life in Jesus Christ. Do you believe what I have testified about Jesus to be true?" "Yes," he humbly replied. I further stated, "Jesus will give you peaceful assurance that you have eternal life. You will never have to worry about death when you welcome Jesus into your heart."

God granted Uncle Chen grace to believe, and he enthusiastically repented and confessed his sins. Then he invited Jesus into his heart to be his Lord and Savior. It was an unbelievable honor to see this cranky old man be filled with divine peace and joy.

Immediately after praying for Uncle Chen, he stated he felt well, and his smile stretched from ear to ear as he arose from his bed. Encouraged by renewed strength, Uncle Chen asked his wife to serve us snacks and drinks. As we ate, we all rejoiced in God's mercy and everlasting love. Uncle Chen's wife was overcome with joy. She expressed that she had never seen her husband with so much peace and happiness. All our hearts were warmed with the presence of God; it was a glorious day. However, our joy changed quickly to sorrow and confusion.

The very next morning, our sons came to give us an update. With broad smiles, they announced they had good news. I expected our sons to tell us that Uncle Chen's entire family had come to Jesus due to his miraculous healing. They were all Buddhists, and his healing would be an incredible testimony! I was wrong.

With glee, they stated, "Uncle Chen died after you prayed for him." I was stunned and confused. I inquired, "How could his death be good news?" Our sons then told us an extraordinary story of what happened after we left Uncle Chen's house.

They recanted, "Shortly after we left Uncle Chen's house, he fell severely ill and was rushed to a nearby hospital by ambulance. His wife immediately contacted all family members and instructed them to hurry to the hospital. As Uncle Chen lay in a comatose state, his family stood nearby shocked, angry, sorrowful, and confused. They had heard the report that their beloved had received a miraculous healing from our prayers. Now, they believed we put a Christian curse on their father. They were outraged with us and our faith. However, God works in mysterious ways. Things are not as they appear."

Our sons continued to share, "In the hospital room, Uncle Chen's family sat quietly waiting for him to perish. Then a bizarre miracle happened. Unexpectedly, Uncle Chen suddenly sat up in his bed. And with a radiant face, he looked up into the heavens and joyfully shouted, "Jesus, I see you, I am coming home." Then he immediately passed!"

Our sons continued to describe what happened next, "Uncle Chen's oldest daughter, an accomplished doctor, stated that they all just witnessed a miracle. She expressed that it was medically impossible for him to instantly come out of a coma and make a pronouncement as he did.Uncle Chen's entire family marveled at what they had just witnessed. They had never seen their beloved one with so much peace and joy. And they could clearly see that Uncle Chen was at peace and knew he was leaving for a better place. Uncle Chen's whole family was in awe of the moment."

And I am convinced that nothing can ever separate us from God's love. Neither death nor life, neither angels nor demons, neither our fears for today nor our worries about tomorrow—not even the powers of hell can separate us from God's love. No power in the sky above or in the earth below—indeed, nothing in all creation will ever be able to separate us from the love of God that is revealed in Christ Jesus our Lord (Romans 8:38-39 NLT).

Then, when our dying bodies have been transformed into bodies that will never die, this Scripture will be fulfilled:

"Death is swallowed up in victory.
O death, where is your victory?
O death, where is your sting?"
(1 Corinthians 15:54-55 NLT)

Reflections

God's thoughts and ways are far superior to ours (see Isaiah 55:8-9). Often, I mistakenly assume God's desired outcome for a particular event. I presumed God would heal Uncle Chen's earthly body through our prayers. However, God had a far superior plan for Uncle Chen—eternal healing. Wonderfully, Uncle Chen received a heavenly body that will never perish. Moreover, Uncle Chen will never experience depression, anxiety, confusion, or strife again. Eternal peace, joy, and love will forever be embracing Uncle Chen!

Moreover, God used the manner of Uncle Chen's passing to be a glorious sign and wonder for his Buddhist family. I have learned that God will work all things together for good to those who love Him (see Romans 8:28).

You may be waiting on God to answer one of your prayers. Don't give up and keep praying until your heart is satisfied (see Luke 18:1). I had an incurable disease. Never losing faith, Kathy prayed until I was healed. She did not listen to my doctor's reports but believed Jesus would heal me. And that is what happened. Five years later, Jesus spoke to me, "Mark, Kathy's faith and prayers have healed you." Immediately, after Jesus made His proclamation, all my horrific symptoms disappeared, and my body was made whole. It was an unbelievable miracle. I am so grateful Kathy did not throw her confidence in Jesus away.

When waiting for a prayer to be answered, keep an open mind. God may not respond in the way you hoped. Uncle Chen received a much greater blessing than we had hoped for. He was ready for heaven (see Romans 8:18). Magnificently, his family was filled with joy seeing their beloved pass on with great peace and happiness.

Jesus Heals a Muslim Woman
in the Marketplace

As I mentioned in a previous story, God gave us a 'mission impossible' assignment. He told us to conduct a revival meeting in the central marketplace in Kota Bharu, the Islamic capital of S.E. Asia. At the time, strife between Muslims and Christians was high. A few radical Muslims had burned and bombed churches over a misunderstanding, making the political and spiritual climate toxic causing Christians to fear persecution. Yet, God's thoughts and ways are far above ours. Amid the unrest, Jesus told us to bring His kingdom to this hard-core Islamic region.

When we entered the market, we started sharing Jesus with some merchants and prayed for those who desired prayer. God reached down with His mighty right hand and performed several miracles, healing several sick and injured people, including a high-ranking retired Muslim police officer. Over the next several years, numerous extraordinary testimonies of God's greatness were birthed from that day; below is one!

The testimonies of the 'Christian God' healing multitudes in the marketplace spread throughout the Muslim community. A homeless mother (Faiza) who had ten children heard about the miraculous healings from a friend, which compelled her to meet us to receive prayer for an injured arm. Her injured arm prevented her from working; she had not worked in two years. Even more tragic, her husband left her and their ten children for another wife. When we met Faiza, she and eight of her children lived with her parents. However, her parents were unsympathetic to their suffering and relegated Faiza and her children to a tiny bedroom. Because there was not enough space on the floor for everyone to lay down, Faiza would sleep, leaning against a wall. Her hardhearted parents also put a padlock on the refrigerator, preventing their grandchildren from eating their food.

Because of the overcrowded living conditions, two of Faiza's older sons were homeless and slept in parks. The two older sons felt their lives had no significance and became depressed and discouraged. To escape their torment, they engaged in a life of alcoholism, drugs, thievery, and violence. When they were hungry, they ate food from garbage cans located in the back alleys of restaurants. Later, after we became acquainted with them, humorously, they recanted their favorite garbage can to eat from was Kentucky Fried Chickens. Wonderfully, God led Kathy and me into their lives, and their dire conditions drastically changed by God's grace.

As I mentioned, getting back to Faiza, we met her through one of her friends. Her friend witnessed our revival meeting in the marketplace a month earlier and told Faiza about all the miraculous healings. Inspired by those testimonies, Faiza asked her friend to set up an appointment with us at a food stall in the same marketplace.

After introductions, Faiza asked Kathy to pray for her injured arm. When Kathy laid her hands on Faiza's arm to pray, Faiza cried out, "I feel needles piercing my arm; what's happening?" I assured her, "Don't be afraid; Jesus is healing you; you are feeling His power." Jesus healed Faiza's arm, and we all rejoiced and thanked God!

Several men were sitting close by. Some were Islamic clerics and observed with more than curiosity. We never know how the Islamic religious authorities will respond to our evangelical efforts, but we press on when we have an audience who wants to hear about Jesus. These men knew we were 'white' missionaries but were overcome with reverence by what they saw and heard. Then these men witnessed something that left them in awe of our God.

God's Spirit came powerfully on Kathy, compelling her to bitterly weep. Kathy could not speak and explain what was happening, so I spoke on her behalf. Compassionately, I said to Faiza, "God created you to be His beloved daughter, and when you hurt, He hurts. God's Spirit lives in Kathy, and He wants you to see how much He cares for you through Kathy's tears and mourning. Kathy is experiencing how God shares your hurts as they were His own.

Once Kathy regained her composure, she shared with Faiza all God had shown her. That was a very tender moment. As Kathy shared many details about her painful past, Faiza wept uncontrollably. Faiza confirmed everything that Kathy stated was true. The Muslim clerics were more overcome by that event than the healing of Faiza's arm. Though they didn't understand what was happening, they were being caught up in God's glory—it was surreal!

The Spirit of the Lord worked powerfully through Kathy that day in the marketplace. Out of Kathy's heart flowed "living waters" (see John 7:38). Consequently, Jesus brought a measure of physical and emotional healing for Faiza.

Faiza lived a life of disgrace and repulsion in the eyes of her family and community. Jesus took Faiza's shame and gave her a double portion of honor. However, Faiza needed more inner healing from her troubled past, which slowly came over the next few years.

Faiza surrendered her life to Jesus on our next visit. Faiza was overcome with joy when she invited Jesus into her heart. What Faiza said shocked us! Jubilantly, she exclaimed, "I feel so different. I don't know how to put it into words except to say I feel like I've been REBORN!" That truth could only come from the Holy Spirit; she had no knowledge of Christian terms.

On our third trip to visit Faiza, she introduced us to her children. Initially, they were suspicious of our motives, but our compassion and good deeds swiftly swept away all apprehension. We rented a place large enough for all the family to comfortably start a new life. We paid for their rent, food, clothes, schooling, and other necessities until they could take care of themselves.

Over the next few months, most of Faiza's older children gave their lives to Jesus, except for her oldest son. Threatened by our Christian faith, he gave us much trouble over the next few years. Eventually, God softened his heart, and now he seeks us for prayer and help. We baptized Faiza and her older children in the ocean. The younger children were not mature enough to make a 'faith' decision on their own accord, so we dedicated them to Jesus. We submerged the older children into the ocean but only poured water over the younger ones.

To help them get on their feet, we gave money to Faiza to start a food stall business next to Kota Bharu's soccer stadium. Faiza is a fantastic cook and did well. When available, we helped her by serving her customers. That allowed us to share the Good News with more Muslims and pray for those who desired prayer.

God strengthened and purified this beautiful family's faith through trials and persecution over the next several years. We walked with them as they endured numerous heart-wrenching troubles - rape, the kidnapping of children, several evictions from their homes, illnesses, and murderous threats. On three occasions, suspicious of their Christian conversion, their landlords evicted them. We always found new places for them.

We are grateful they were never arrested and jailed for their faith. God never takes pleasure when evil brings harm to His children. However, darkness still invades the earth and harms righteous and unrighteous people. Gratefully, whatever Satan means for destruction, God will bring restoration and beauty for those who love and trust Him.

In Malaysian culture, every clan has a designated patriarch who oversees crucial decisions. They appointed me to be their lifelong patriarch. I am deeply honored, but I also take this role seriously. Trouble seems to always follow this clan, which keeps us on our knees.

Several months after Faiza gave her life to Jesus, she called to share devastating news. Faiza cried out, "Dad, I need to see you and mom right away. Something horrible has happened to me." She wouldn't tell us over the phone what happened, but she wouldn't stop crying, so we knew her trouble was severe. We canceled our appointments for the next two days to love on her.

Faiza arrived by bus early the following day. When we settled in our house, we asked Faiza what caused her so much distress. Tearfully, she responded, "I was raped, and now I am pregnant. My life is over. I tried to commit suicide by digesting poison; I wanted to go and be with Jesus. But Jesus intervened and said, 'Go see your spiritual parents, they will know what to do.'" Faiza's grief became ours, and we wept with her. However, godly mourning doesn't remain in a place of despair and hopelessness; it seeks God for healing, restoration, and comfort. In Jesus, we will always find comfort from our troubles (see Matthew 5:4).

Faiza informed us that according to Malaysian law if she could not prove who the father was, she would be labeled a whore and sent to prison.

And her newborn child will be labeled a bastard, won't get a national I.D. card, and immediately sent to a horrible institution. She further stated that the hospital authorities would require her to fill out a form asking for the father's name.

We informed Faiza that she was God's precious daughter and that if she followed God's ways, He would do a miracle, and those things would not happen. She cried, "I only trust Jesus and you and mom. What must I do? Kathy shared her experience of being raped and how Jesus healed her of all painful memories and restored her. Kathy shared she forgave her rapist and trusted God to bring good from that horrible moment. And He did, abundantly!

Comforted by Kathy's testimony, Faiza got on her knees with us and forgave her rapist. She was brokenhearted and sincere in her forgiveness. There were a lot of tears but also hope that God would bring good out of her suffering. We told Faiza we would meet her at the hospital the day she gave birth.

After her baby boy (Daniel) was born, she was brought to a large room that served many other patients. Immediately, Faiza was asked to fill out a form. She left blank on the form the father's name and anxiously waited for a response from the hospital authorities.

We met Faiza in this large room a few hours after she gave birth. Faiza greeted us with jubilance. She said, "Everyone in the hospital showed me, love, even knowing that my baby was the result of rape. Daniel was not labeled a bastard and received his National I.D. card. I'm shocked and grateful; I don't believe that has ever happened in Malaysia before. I won't be going to prison, and Daniel won't be going to a horrible institution." We cried, rejoiced, and gave thanks to Jesus.

Filled with love and gratefulness for Jesus, Faiza asked me to perform a dedication in the presence of all the Muslims in the large room. She said, "Dad, I want to dedicate Daniel to Jesus. Would you hold Daniel up high and give him to Jesus? "All in the room watched as I held Daniel above my head and declared that he belonged to Jesus. Surprisingly, everyone watched in awe. They knew we were Christians. It didn't matter; God filled the room with His glory, touching all present.

As I write this story, Daniel is now ten years old, and everyone who knows him states he's a remarkable boy filled with God's grace.

Faiza and her family will always have a special place in our hearts. While we lived in Malaysia, we spent much time with them - establishing businesses, celebrating holidays and birthdays, but most importantly, enjoying life with them. Even now, through social media, we remain fully engaged in their lives. On our return trips to Malaysia, they always meet us with tears, long embraces, and lots of kisses. They knew our love, respect, and honor to be genuine. We will forever cherish our relationship with this beautiful family.

They have become courageous and bold in their faith. Discarding any fear of persecution, they fearlessly share their faith with friends and acquaintances. They affectionately tell us, "We want to be brave for Jesus like you both!" And they most definitely are!

Testimonies of God's healing power spread throughout a Muslim region. A Muslim woman, who heard the reports, sought to investigate to see if they were real. In her pursuit, she and her family found salvation.

And God confirmed the message by giving signs and wonders and various miracles and gifts of the Holy Spirit whenever he chose (Hebrews 2:4 NLT).

Reflections

A single act of obedience can be the seed that starts an unstoppable revival. Amid the Islamic uprising, we preached God's Word to many radical Muslims. Wonderfully, God confirmed our message with miraculous signs and wonders. As a result, God removed the veil from many eyes that kept them from clearly seeing Jesus for who He is. To this day, the Kingdom of God is advancing in Kota Bahru.

Initially, we were fearful to obey God, but we strengthened ourselves in His Spirit and submitted. Consequently, God gave us boldness and courage to unabashedly preach the Good News to those who strongly opposed Christianity. As a result, Faiza, her family, and many other Muslims found salvation in Jesus. They have become monuments of God's grace in their communities. God is able and willing to empower His children so that they can reveal His glory in impossible situations.

Perhaps God is calling you to be His representative in your family or community. Maybe the situation looks impossible. Maybe you feel unqualified. Perhaps you are scared. If so, don't lose heart; you are human. Wait on the Lord, and He will give you divine strength. He will give you eagle wings to soar to new heights. You will run and not get weary (see Isaiah 40:31).

Moreover, He will make the impossible possible (see Mark 10:27). Furthermore, God will give you "revival seeds" to plant in your family, community, and anywhere He sends you. And most assuredly, a harvest of righteousness will come from your efforts, bringing glory to God.

A Perilous Rescue Saves
Two Young Sisters

Most missionary work cannot be taught in a classroom. Heavenly Father sent the Holy Spirit in Jesus' Name to teach, encourage, and guide us. I have had no better teacher of doing missions than the Holy Spirit. Despite our shortcomings and character flaws, we can always be hopeful for a good outcome because we have God's Spirit living in our vessels. And the Holy Spirit is always able to make impossible situations possible, no matter how dangerous and dire our circumstances. We only need to believe in Jesus and be led by the Holy Spirit to make it so.

"But the Helper, the Holy Spirit, whom the Father will send in my name, he will teach you all things and bring to your remembrance all that I have said to you" (John 14:26 EVS).

These truths exemplify how two young sisters were rescued from their violent father and uncle, drug addicts. We met with a family we had been discipling in the teachings of Jesus. Our love for them, and theirs for us, was deep and beautiful. They always greeted us with many long embraces, kisses, and broad smiles. Not on this day. When we entered their home, the climate was as if we came to a funeral procession.

I inquired why everyone was so sullen and downcast. Rebekah, one of our spiritual daughters, started to wail. Her countenance shouted utter fear. Rebekah cried out, "My husband and his brother kidnapped my daughters. They are violent drug addicts; recently, my husband stabbed his mother with a knife. He has hidden my daughters, and I haven't seen them in over two weeks." She was hysterical! Her daughters were only two and three years old.

Faith rose up in me, and I confidently declared, "God will bring your daughters back home today. Let's pray for His guidance and wisdom." "God can't help with this matter," Rebekah retorted. Wanting to give her hope, I gently replied, "I will pray silently, and God will give me a plan to find and save your daughters." Gratefully, God gave me specific instructions on what to do next, which I shared with Rebekah and her family.

I shared, "God wants us to file a report at the police station. He will give you favor with the police, and they will help us find your daughters. In complete disgust, Rebekah snapped, "Grandpa, you do not know our culture! Being a woman, I will get into serious trouble if I accuse a man of wrongdoing. We are governed by Shariah law." Not relenting, I softly responded, "I know your culture very well. But, as Christians, we live in a different kingdom that is superior to all human cultures. Jesus is King of this new kingdom, and if our ways please Him, He will give us favor and victory. We only need to believe and obey." I reminded Rebekah of all the miracles Jesus had done in their lives, hoping that would persuade her.

She was encouraged, and along with her mother and two siblings, we went to a local police station. Sobbing, Rebekah told her story to the police. They compassionately responded by saying they would help find her daughters. The policemen set aside their cultural ways to do the right thing. I quietly thanked Jesus for giving us unusual favor.

They asked Rebekah to lead them to her in-law's house, hoping her husband's parents or siblings would help locate her daughters.

Once we arrived at the in-law's house, the police told us to stay outside because it might get violent. After some loud shouting and what sounded like furniture being knocked around, Rebekah's sister-in-law came out with the police, forcing her to lead us to Rebekah's husband's hideout.

Rebekah and her family climbed into our car. We then followed the police and Rebekah's sister-in-law, who were all on separate motorbikes, to a dense jungle area outside of city limits.

We drove a few miles down a narrow road through the jungle and stopped. Rebekah's sister-in-law pointed to a large chicken coop elevated about five feet off the ground and said, "You will find them in the chicken coop."

Not waiting for the police to make a move, Rebekah angrily climbed the chicken coop ladder and flung open the door. Horrified by what she saw, Rebekah screamed! Her daughters were crying, covered in dirt, and frightened. Rebekah was furious and immediately engaged in a fight with her husband, hoping to subdue him and rescue her daughters. She failed; her husband overpowered her and threw her down the ladder. He shouted, "The girls stay with me."

I was praying and hoping the police would help, but they stood frozen in fear and refused to respond. I knew the father and his brother were addicted to horse tranquilizers, making them psychotic and violent. Also, he could be raping his own daughters. Knowing this, I pleaded with the policemen to help—they would not. They said their part in rescuing the girls was done. I was furious with their lack of compassion. Seeking God's guidance, the Holy Spirit said, "Mark, go and subdue the father and rescue those girls. I will be with you."

I knew if I proceeded, there was a strong possibility the police would shoot me for fighting a Muslim. It was a cardinal offense for a Christian to attack a Muslim. I wasn't deterred; I could never live with myself for not trying. Love would not let me remain silent and watch. Though I was over fifty years old, and the drug addict father was in his mid-twenties, I trusted God would be with me.

I quickly climbed the steps to the chicken coop and put a good-ole-fashion headlock on the father. As I was dragging him out of the chicken coop, he was screaming at the policemen, "Shoot the white man." I responded and said to the police, "Though it doesn't look like it, I love this man. But he is dangerous to his daughters, and I must return them to their mother until he changes his ways. If he lets me, I will help him to be a better father." The father's brother sat motionlessly and gave me no trouble. And, gratefully, the police did not shoot or arrest me. I know God's angels were helping.

I contained the father in a headlock until Kathy secured the sisters in our car. Once I saw them safe, I released the father, and he gave me no further trouble. The police appeared satisfied with the outcome and allowed us to depart. We were tremendously grateful and relieved!

The girls were severely traumatized. So, we spent the rest of the day loving them. We fed them, washed them, bought them cute new dresses, and took them to a beautiful ocean beach to play with some new toys—all that same day. By the end of the day, the girls were happy and exhausted! So was everyone else!

Love never gives up and always finds a way. That day, against all odds, love found a way to rescue two beautiful young girls from their violent, drug addict father and uncle. All things are possible with God for those who love and trust Him!

"And he will answer, 'I tell you the truth, when you refused to help the least of these my brothers and sisters, you were refusing to help me"
(Matthew 25:45 NLT).

But you will receive power when the Holy Spirit has come upon you, and you will be my witnesses in Jerusalem and in all Judea and Samaria, and to the end of the earth" (Acts 1:8 ESV).

Reflections

Jesus came to give abundant life overflowing with joy, peace, and righteousness (see John 10:10). However, it is not easy to see God's goodness when we are amidst a horrendous trial. The devil, an opportunist, will attempt to steal our blessings and destroy our hope when we appear vulnerable (see John 10:10). However, these trials can be opportunities for indescribable joy and greater faith if we don't throw away our confidence in Jesus amid our troubles (see James 1:2-4). We only need to stay close to Jesus to make it so.

Rebekah was hopeless and tormented by a spirit of fear. Thoughts of her daughter's destruction loomed in her imagination. The devil had his way with Rebekah. However, God is willing and able to bring beauty from ashes, joy instead of mourning, and festive praise instead of despair (see Isaiah 61:3).

God is never surprised when troubles and trials come our way; He's eternal. Therefore, He always has a plan for victory. No matter how dire our situation, God has a plan for us to be victorious. The "Cross of Calvary" makes us Victors and not victims. Gratefully, Rebekah trusted my leadership. Consequently, she received a glorious reward for her faith. We found and rescued her daughters from their violent, drug addict father and uncle.

Perhaps you are amid a seemingly impossible trial. Do not throw away your confidence in Jesus, which is more precious than gold. Instead, persevere in prayer and faith until you receive the glory of your hope (see Hebrews 10:35-36). You will never be ashamed for fully trusting Jesus! My trials have been the best soil for my faith to grow to new heights.

Coffee Habit Leads to a Revival at a Muslim Wedding

Coffee is my all-time favorite beverage! You might disagree, but I believe coffee is a marvelous gift from God. Admittingly, I have a caffeine dependency. But nevertheless, God can do amazing things through our weaknesses; He is full of grace and mercy. This story is about how God used my coffee habit to shine His glory at a Muslim wedding. It's amazing how God works all things together for good for those who are called according to His purpose (see Romans 8:28).

We planned to travel from Kota Bharu to Gua Musang, two cities in northern Malaysia. One of our disciples lived in Gua Musang. We were eager to see her and her children; we loved them deeply. We departed Kota Bharu early morning before the food stalls opened. I reasoned I would find coffee at a roadside food stall along the way. However, I forgot, it was Ramadan - Muslims holy month. And by Islamic law, Muslims are forbidden to eat or drink from sunrise to sunset during Ramadan. Consequently, there were no food stalls open.

After an hour of traveling on a road that meandered through forested terrain, I saw a Muslim man sitting in front of his house. It might sound strange, but I was prompted to stop and ask him if he would make a pot of coffee for my team and me. I reasoned that I would offer to pay him generously. And I would initiate a conversation about religion while I drank my coffee. Most Muslims enjoy engaging in those conversations. If he didn't have coffee, and if he was willing, I would still offer to pray a blessing over him.

After introductions, I asked this kind man (Mohamed) if I could pay him to make a pot of coffee. Praise God, he offered to brew a fresh pot just for us, even though he could not have any. It was a glorious morning chatting with Mohamed; he was talkative, congenial, and humorous. Before we left, I asked if we could pray a blessing over him. I call this 'prayer blessing evangelism, which often leads to more ministry. When a person allows me to bless them in the Name of Jesus, the Holy Spirit always touches them. If they seek healing and don't get healed, they are still profoundly touched by God's peace and love.

Mohamed eagerly accepted my invitation for prayer. Like I always do, before I prayed, I shared with Mohamed who Jesus is and why He came into this world. I told him that Jesus loves Muslims, and so do we! And that Jesus desired to reveal His love.

When I laid my hand on Mohamed's shoulder and prayed, God's presence overcame him. For a long moment, Mohamed sat motionless, experiencing God's glory. Astonished by what he was encountering, Mohamed yelled for his wife to come out of their house to meet us. Mohamed wanted us to pray for her; she was ill. She came, and Kathy prayed for her. Mohamed's wife was overcome by God's glory in the same manner as him. They both looked at us, thinking, "Who are these people that possess such power in their prayers." What came next blew our minds!

Inspired by our prayers, Mohamed asked if we would come back to his house before noon that Friday. He gave no reason except to say there would be many people present. Though it's a six-hour drive, there was no way we would miss this God-given opportunity to preach the message of salvation to multitudes of Muslims.

Upon arrival, we were met by a crowd that gathered in front of Mohamed's house. The occasion was a wedding ceremony; his oldest son was getting married. Mohamed approached me and quietly said, "Thank you for coming. I have a favor to ask. After the Imam performs the wedding ritual, would you both be willing to pray a blessing over my son and daughter-in-law? When the Imam prays, there is no power. But when you both pray, there is much power, and we want God's blessings on their marriage." What an astonishing request from a Muslim father in a staunch Islamic region! We eagerly agreed to do so! We felt incredibly honored.

We not only prayed for the newlyweds, but we also prayed for almost everyone who attended the wedding. One precious moment was when all the girls sat on the floor, hanging on Kathy's every word while she spoke about Jesus. Also, Kathy prayed for several women to be healed of various illnesses. Meanwhile, I prayed for the men. Not one person opposed us as we shared the Gospel of Salvation. It was a glorious and unforgettable day.

We remained friends with a few family members and other locals for many years. We shared testimonies about God's goodness and bible stories relevant to their lives. And we always prayed for them on every visit. They all loved hearing about Jesus. And I genuinely believe many came to believe Jesus is God's Son who came to save the world from their sins. But fear kept them from making decisions to be Christ's disciples.

Their son and daughter-in-law moved to a city about an hour from where we lived. We visited them often. One day, they called us and asked if we would come to their house; they requested prayer over an urgent matter. Upon arrival, they informed us that it would take a miracle for her to get pregnant. She got pregnant shortly after we prayed. Encouraged by God's loving blessing, she gave her life to Jesus! Sadly, her husband had been seduced by a Muslim mafia gang and had become a member. Gratefully, he allowed his wife to be a Christian without persecuting her. I know he feared our God!

As a result of stopping for a cup of coffee, Kingdom seeds were planted into many hearts, and a beautiful soul found salvation. Perhaps others will be saved later. Perhaps the seeds of truth will set them free.

"I tell you the truth, anyone who believes in me will do the same works I have done, and even greater works, because I am going to be with the Father. You can ask for anything in my name, and I will do it, so that the Son can bring glory to the Father. Yes, ask me for anything in my name, and I will do it," (John 14:12-14 NLT)!

Reflections

God's presence is powerfully felt through prayers. I learned this when I first met Kathy back in 1985. She wasn't a Christian but allowed me to pray blessings over her. When I would place my hand on her and pray, she cried. I know God was overcoming Kathy with His love and pleasure. Kathy surrendered her life a few months after we met.

After we got married, we made it a practice to pray for whoever desired prayer. We call this "prayer blessing evangelism." We owned a business and frequently offered to pray for our clients. We have multitudes of glorious testimonies for doing so.

Moreover, by Holy Spirit's prompting, we would offer to pray for strangers in restaurants, grocery stores, malls, and everywhere we went. When approaching someone, we would say, "This might sound crazy, but we believe God led us to you for a reason. We are Christians and believe in the power of prayer.Is there something you are hoping for in your life that has not come? We would love to pray for anything that is on your heart." A vast majority of people graciously consent to receive our prayers, no matter their faith or beliefs. Sometimes, God gives us a "Word of Knowledge." When He does, lives are turned upside down!

Not everyone receives healing from our prayers, at least not immediately. But most expressed unusual peace overcame them when we prayed.

Mohamed and his wife were profoundly moved by experiencing God's pleasure after we laid our hands on them and prayed. Desiring that their children and village have the same experience, they invited us to their son's wedding. That was astounding! They were devout Muslims and clearly knew we were Christians. They took a grave risk inviting us.Nevertheless, their courage led to miraculous healings and salvations.

If you are a "Believer," God will use you in the same fashion He does us. You have the same Holy Spirit as any other Believer. I advise you to keep it simple. When led by Holy Spirit, tell those you meet God loves them and wants to bless them. Ask them if they would like prayer for something, such as healing for themselves or someone they know. Most people will respond respectfully with genuine and sincere requests. Often this can lead to sharing your testimony about what Jesus has done for you. Always keep love as your highest goal, and God will use you to touch others powerfully.

Mute Indonesian Woman
Speaks for the First Time

A Lutheran Church located in Medan, Indonesia, invited us to conduct a healing/revival service. We were informed they were traditional in their faith and had never hosted a charismatic meeting. The senior pastor opposed such events and was fearful they would set a precedence of spiritual chaos. However, one of his associate pastors finally convinced him to host a revival meeting; and that took 20 years of debate. The associate pastor believed God still moved in miracles, and he desperately wanted their flock to experience God's supernatural power.

The associate pastor heard about our mission work in Malaysia through a mutual Indonesian acquaintance. He was told that an elderly couple, Lutheran missionaries, won multitudes of Muslims in Malaysia for Jesus through bold testimony and miraculous signs and wonders. He used our testimony to persuade his lead pastor to invite us to conduct a healing/revival service in their church. However, the senior pastor remained nervous and even suspicious of our ministry.

I'm not sure how the associate pastor concluded we were Lutheran missionaries; we never presented ourselves as such. Perhaps he googled us and saw we were former pastors at a Lutheran Church in Lakeville, Minnesota. Nevertheless, that information convinced his senior pastor to give us an invitation. We no longer identify with any denomination because we believe it's best to represent Christ's kingdom, as expressed in the Bible, without denominational leanings with those of other faiths and beliefs.

Indonesia has the largest Muslim population globally. Like Malaysia, Indonesian Christians represent a small minority and fear evangelizing the

Muslims. Receiving invitations to preach and teach in their churches were excellent opportunities to encourage the pastors and their congregations to reach out to their Muslim neighbors.

We enthusiastically accepted their invitation, knowing God would pour out His Spirit and perform miracles in this quaint Indonesian Lutheran church. Moreover, I felt honored that God appointed me to conduct this service at this historic time in their church. So, at least I thought I was God's choice.

When we arrived at the church, hungry souls packed the place, hoping to receive a divine touch from God. They were expectant God was going to visit them. There was not enough room for everyone to sit, so multitudes gathered outside, looking through the church front door and open church windows. The expressions of those outside brought us to tears; they did not want God to overlook them because they could not be seated in the church.

The atmosphere was electric with faith! It was evident that many prayers had prepared a way for a divine encounter. The first few rows were filled with sick, injured, and demonically tormented souls, hoping to be healed. This was unbelievable for a Lutheran church that had never had a charismatic meeting to have such incredible faith. They were a magnet for God's glory to invade their meeting. I was excited to preach!

Kathy and I sat upfront with the senior pastor and two of his associate pastors. It's customary in the Indonesian churches for all pastors and guest speakers to wear suits and ties. With no air-conditioners present, I was saturated in sweat within the first minute. Did not matter; I was overflowing with joy and expectancy!

As everyone worshiped, profound love for God filled the atmosphere. And God did not disappoint their desperate cries for a divine encounter. We were humbled by what we saw and heard.

When the lead pastor arose to introduce me, I could barely contain my excitement. But as he was approaching the podium, Jesus spoke to me, "Mark, I have not anointed you to speak; I have anointed Kathy!" Whoa, everyone was expecting me, and women were not permitted to speak at this church. However, I have learned that humility, obedience, and honor are required to host God's presence. And if I did not comply, I knew it would not go well.

So, I quickly turned to Kathy and told her God had anointed her and not me to speak and asked if she had a message. "Yes, I have a message," she replied. This would be an awkward moment knowing women were not allowed to preach in this church. Furthermore, everyone was expecting me.

After the senior pastor introduced and invited me to come forward, Kathy arose and proceeded upfront. Suddenly the room became eerily quiet; you could hear a pin drop. Kathy stated later that she could hear her heart beating with every step she took towards the podium.

Once upfront, Kathy did not explain why she was preaching and not me; she immediately started to preach. And it was evident to all present that Kathy was preaching by the Spirit of God. Suddenly, heaven's glory flooded the room, and everyone sensed it. Satan, wanting to pervert God's plans, provoked a man to manifest. The man arose and started to scream with a demonically distorted face. Discerning a demon spoke through this man, Kathy rebuked the evil spirit and told the man to sit down. Immediately, he complied.

Kathy's sermon was powerful; it encouraged everyone's faith to soar to new heights. After her message, Kathy asked those who wanted prayer to come forward. Though this church had never conducted an altar call, there was a mad rush to the front. Not wanting to be left out, people became undignified and shoved one another to secure a front-line spot for prayer. We have experienced this type of desperation many times in foreign countries. That type of hunger always pleases God!

Interpreters had been assigned to assist both Kathy and me. A mother brought her twenty-year-old daughter for prayer. I asked the mother how I could pray for them. With an anguished plea, she stated, "Please pray for my daughter's healing." "What's wrong with her," I asked? Her daughter was beautiful, and she had a pleasant demeanor and appeared healthy. "She has never spoken a word from birth," the mother replied sadly.

The senior pastor was standing behind me - he was restless. I could feel his breath on the backside of my neck. He loved his church as a father loves his family and did not want anything to manifest in his church that wasn't from God. I had compassion and understood his attitude - I came from a Lutheran background that opposed the charismatic movement. I held the same sentiments about the charismatic gifts until God opened my eyes through several miraculous and bizarre events.

The senior pastor said, "It's true; I know her well. I baptized her when she was an infant, and I have never heard her speak a word." He also stated that there was no medical explanation for why she couldn't speak.

I told the mother and her daughter that I would ask Jesus how to proceed.

Jesus often speaks to me through scripture, and He did so this time. Jesus brought the following scripture to my mind: When they left, a demon-possessed man who couldn't speak was brought to Jesus. So Jesus cast out the demon, and then the man began to speak. The crowds were amazed. "Nothing like this has ever happened in Israel!" they exclaimed (Matthew 9:32-33 NLT).

Jesus told me to cast the demon out of the young woman and that she would be able to speak immediately. When I shared this with the mother and her daughter, my Interpreter refused to translate my message. He told me he didn't want to get their hopes up only to be disappointed. I admonished him for his lack of faith, "You have become a barrier to God's will. God will do this miracle without you translating."

Trusting the Holy Spirit, I commanded the demon to leave in Jesus' Name. Then, trusting God, I instructed the daughter to repeat the following words after me, "Jesus loves me, and I love Jesus." With no hesitation and perfect clarity, the young woman cheerfully repeated those very words - in English. We all cried and praised God for this incredible miracle.

Then the senior pastor did the very thing he was afraid might happen. He jumped up and down like a crazy man shouting with exuberance. He could not contain himself. He grabbed the microphone and testified to his church of God's wondrous miracle. He then asked, "Would you like Mark & Kathy to come back again?" With a thunderous response, they replied, "Yes, please invite them to come again." Oh, God is so good and so faithful to show His love to the broken-hearted and hungry.

Others that glorious day received miraculous healings, but not all. For those that didn't, we wept with them. We rejoice with those who celebrate and mourn with those in sorrow. But I must add that our tears and compassion always comfort those who don't receive immediate healing. And we always encourage them to continue to pray until God answers their prayers.

> *Look, I have given you authority over all the power of the enemy, and you can walk among snakes and scorpions and crush them. Nothing will injure you. But don't rejoice because evil spirits obey you; rejoice because your names are registered in heaven" (Luke 10:19-20—NLT).*

Reflections

When God gives us instructions, we rarely see the entirety of His plan or fully understand His purposes. This keeps us from getting prideful. Instead, it keeps us in a posture of humility, which is required to receive ongoing grace (see James 4:6).

I believed God called me to preach to the Indonesian church. My belief was understandable since the Indonesian church did not allow women to preach. However, God wanted to demonstrate that He uses women powerfully to fulfill His purposes. Because Kathy and I remained humble and obedient, God reached down with His mighty right hand and performed many miracles—most notably delivering the young Indonesian woman from a mute spirit.

It is not wise to say, "I know God's perfect plan." Instead, it is wise to say, "God has given me a vision of His plans and purposes. I cannot see it fully, but as I seek His wisdom, God will bring clarity" (see James 4:13). Humility is a magnet for God's presence. Always strive to remain humble under God's mighty power, and He will exalt you in proper time (see 1 Peter 5:6).

Revival on an Indonesian Ferryboat

After a couple of years living in Malaysia, our reputation for winning Muslims for Jesus had reached Indonesia. Encouraged by reports of our success, an Indonesian pastor located in Medan, Sumatra, Indonesia, invited us to conduct an evangelism workshop for Indonesian pastors and Christian leaders. This was a momentous shift - fear of persecution and resentment towards Muslims hindered their efforts from evangelizing Muslims. Indonesia has the world's largest population of Muslims, and they control the Government. Besides the workshop, our host pastor set up many revival/healing crusades for us - indoor and outdoor in the surrounding cities and villages.

About one hundred pastors and Christian leaders came to our evangelism workshop to learn spiritual principles that would empower them to reach Muslims for Jesus. I sensed their intentions were pure, and they sincerely wanted to change their attitudes towards Muslim outreach. Like most pastors, they relied too heavily on intellectualism, neglecting their trust in God's power. That day, God changed their hearts and approach.

During my presentation, I continuously declared we need the baptism of the Holy Spirit to receive power to be effective witnesses for Jesus (see Acts 1:8).I shared several supporting scripture and numerous testimonies of how God used us to reach Muslims in Malaysia. We also showed slides of our Malaysian ministry, confirming our testimonies.

After my presentation, I asked if anyone desired to have a fresh baptism of the Holy Spirit. All the pastors stood up, and when I prayed for the Holy Spirit to come, most fell on the floor by the power of God's Spirit. This was amazing because they were mainstream pastors, not Charismatic or Pentecostal.

Several pastors wanted to learn by example, so they followed us to the villages where we conducted crusades. God poured out His Spirit on all our gatherings - multitudes received salvation, deliverance, and healing. I could write another book about the numerous unusual occurrences at our campaigns.

On this mission trip to Indonesia, we traveled to Samosir Island, located on Lake Toba. The region is populated mainly by the Batak tribe. Samosir Island is one of the largest lake islands in the world—243 square miles.In my opinion, Lake Toba is the most beautiful lake globally. It stretches 60 miles long and 19 miles wide and rests in a gigantic volcanic depression. Steep mountainous peaks stretch towards the sky surrounding the entire lake.

Most of the Batak tribe had returned to their pagan beliefs. The majority had built large shrines to worship their dead ancestors. Many of their shrines cost more than their houses. Sadly, they conducted pagan rituals on Sundays rather than attending church. Consequently, their syncretic behavior (mixing religious beliefs with pagan practices that oppose one another) opened the door for demonic activity.

Most of the Batak people were oppressed and tormented. Our mission was to conduct numerous open-air campaigns in their villages to revive and strengthen their faith in Jesus. Also, to meet with and encourage the Batak pastors privately. However, God instructed me to warn the pastors of the consequences of allowing their congregants to worship their dead ancestors. Healing and restoration would only come through confession and repentance of those sins.

The only way to get to the island is by ferryboat, which takes over an hour. As soon as our ferryboat departed from the dock, God gave me instructions to conduct a revival meeting—on the ferryboat. And I had one hour to do so.God wanted to demonstrate to the Indonesian pastors accompanying us that He can do great things anytime we believe and obey His voice.

The Holy Spirit guided my attention to three impoverished young boys from the Batak tribe. They were selling newspapers to the passengers and needed the profits to survive.Non-stop, they shouted their promotion—desperate to get money to buy food for themselves and their families.

The Holy Spirit compelled me to buy all their papers and give them three times what they were asking. I was instructed to hand out all the newspapers to the passengers, free of charge. And while handing out the papers, I was to invite anyone desiring prayers to come to the center of the boat. I told the passengers my wife would be waiting to pray for whoever wanted prayer.

The Batak boys were overcome by my gesture to give significantly more than they asked. Having their undivided attention, I shared the gospel of salvation. I also shared many beautiful testimonies of how Jesus saved me from my sins and transformed me for His glory.

I then asked the Batak boys if they wanted to invite Jesus into their hearts to be their Lord and Savior. They enthusiastically accepted. It was a tender and precious moment. They were overcome with emotion when they received Jesus. I was humbled by their sincerity.

Our Interpreter was a Batak and worship leader who had brought his guitar. I asked him to teach the teenage boys a worship song in their language. He did, and we were all shocked by what happened next.

God's Spirit fell upon the Batak boys; when they opened their mouths to sing, they sounded like angels from heaven. Their voices were beautiful. As they sang, I could hear a cry emerge from their hearts to commune with God. I got goosebumps all over my body. Some of us heard glorious singing from invisible sources. We are convinced they were angels. Everyone witnessing this event was mesmerized.

As I handed out all the newspapers to the passengers, I invited them to go to the middle of the ferryboat, where Kathy would pray for them. Some passengers accepted my invitation, left their vehicles, and sought Kathy for prayer.

Others were overcome by the worship and left their cars to join in. It was a surreal sight; Christians, Muslims, and Buddhists had gathered to dance and sing Christian songs with the Batak boys. God's glory pierced through the darkness, and Jesus was glorified.

A Muslim man from Bandar Ache, one of the most radical Islamic cities globally, joined us in worship. With abandoned glee, he locked arms with me, and, together, we joyfully sang and danced. When the Spirit of God moves, impossibilities become possible.

I never experienced worship that glorious as on that ferryboat to Samosir Island. The Indonesian pastors who accompanied us were both amazed and encouraged. It was a precious, tender moment that we will never forget. God reached down and honored the impoverished Batak boys. Their identities swiftly changed from being nobodies to being significant. Only God's power can transform someone that quickly. They felt dignified, and their smiles stretched from ear to ear. In one glorious moment, Jesus delivered the boys from the kingdom of darkness to the kingdom of light, and most on the ferry rejoiced in God's glorious presence, Christians, Muslims, and Buddhists.

Our mission was waiting for us on Samosir Island. That is another incredible testimony of God's faithfulness. However, sometimes God arranges detours on our journey. We just need to be ready and obey.

The heart of man plans his way, but the LORD establishes his steps
(Proverbs 16:9 - ESV).

Reflections

Before I received the baptism of the Holy Spirit, my evangelism efforts were moderately successful. That changed when Randy Clark, a worldwide renowned revivalist, prayed for me to receive the glorious baptism of the Holy Spirit. Since then, my evangelical efforts have led to a much greater harvest of souls (see Acts 1:8).

Over one hundred Indonesian pastors and leaders came to our conference to hear how God used Kathy and me to bring Muslims to salvation. They were expecting us to teach methods derived from carnal wisdom. Instead, we shared biblical principles for evangelism.

We instructed the pastors and leaders to keep their message simple. And to rely on God's power and not humanistic methods so that Muslims would put their faith in God's power and not carnal wisdom (see 1 Corinthians 2:1-5). Moreover, we encouraged them to always testify to why Jesus had to die and the significance of His resurrection. We encouraged them to always share their personal testimony and why they trust and love Jesus. Our testimony will be weak if lost souls cannot clearly see our love and reverence for Christ.

We emphasized never to preach a compromised message to appease Muslims. Too many missionaries do so, perverting Christ's Gospel of Salvation. They allow a spirit of intimidation to pervert their witness. Holy Spirit will never convict hearts when the Gospel of Salvation is preached with intentional errors. Muslims will only see Jesus clearly when the Holy Spirit removes the veils that keep them blind from the truth. We can never convict anyone of truth; only Holy Spirit can. And when we preach boldly in truth, accompanied with compassion, the Holy Spirit will move with power.

All the attendees believed our testimonies and asked to receive the gift of the Holy Spirit. God graciously saw their hunger, and consequently, they all fell to the floor when the Holy Spirit came upon them. God confirmed the importance of being baptized in the Holy Spirit at all our meetings, including the ferryboat.

We were tremendously honored and blessed to be part of God's excellent plan to encourage the Indonesian pastors and leaders. And mostly to bring salvation to many precious souls.

The baptism of the Holy Spirit is for every Believer. If you have not received this marvelous baptism, earnestly seek it with all your heart and with utmost reverence for God. God's unmerited favor is for all his children, not just a select few. Your education, race, gender, social status, or experiences are inconsequential in your witnessing efforts. We all need the Holy Spirit's baptism to receive power to be effective witnesses for Jesus (see Acts 1:8).

Indonesian "Hitman" Finds Salvation

As I have mentioned, while serving as missionaries in Malaysia, Kathy and I received ongoing invitations from Indonesian pastors to conduct healing/revival meetings in their country. We could not accept all their invitations because our mission work in Malaysia required our full attention. However, when prompted by the Holy Spirit, we conducted both open-air and indoor crusades on Sulawesi, Sumatra, and Java islands over the years.

A Malaysian pastor, and close friend, made frequent mission trips to Java, Indonesia. He invited us to accompany him on one of his trips to Jakarta, Indonesia's capital. He had prearranged for us to preach at several different churches.

A church located on Jakarta's outskirts invited us to conduct a healing/revival meeting. Prompted by the Holy Spirit, I preached on the "Blood of Jesus." I was a dreadful sinner in my earlier years but powerfully experienced the cleansing power of 'Christ's Blood!' So, I was always eager to preach on that topic. Moreover, I believe everyone needs to be reminded about God's unfathomable mercy shown through the sacrifice of His Son. This Sunday, God brought a distraught man who needed to hear this message—his life was on the line.

Having been deeply touched by God's love, I always preach from a place of deep gratitude. I once felt filthy and shameful because of my sinful nature. Washed by the precious Blood of Jesus, I could now stand before congregations and preach with conviction and authority. What an incredible honor God has bestowed on me to preach around the world about His amazing grace and mercy.

That Sunday, I implored all who would listen to believe that the "Blood of Jesus" has the power to wash away all their sin, guilt, and shame. I declared,

"Even if you have murdered many people, God will wash away your sins and make you as white as snow. And His grace is freely given to anyone who believes in Jesus and confesses and repents of their sins."

With tears running down my face, I shared my testimony with the congregation: "I was once the worst of sinners. I was a wretched man; shame, guilt, and self-condemnation tormented me continuously. I had come to a place of hopelessness and utter despair. I believed a happy, productive life was no longer attainable. Overwhelmed with misery and no hope for happiness, I planned my suicide."

I further shared, "Wonderfully, Jesus met me with mercy and compassion just before I was about to end my life. Jesus stated, 'Mark, if you follow me, I will lead you into abundant life.' I didn't know if that was my imagination or really Jesus speaking to me. So, I inquired, 'Jesus, I will surrender my life to you if you are real. But I need confirmation; I don't want to follow a false imagination and waste my time. All I want is peace. If you give me this one thing, I will do whatever you say and go wherever you send me the rest of my life.'

I continued with my testimony, "Jesus beautifully answered my prayer. His glory came over me, and I felt strangely peaceful. All my fears and hopelessness strangely washed away. I was experiencing God's mercy powerfully. I was not capable of conjuring up these tranquil feelings. I had no doubt God had wonderfully touched me with His majestic love.

Overwhelmed by God's tenderness, I repented of my evil ways, confessed my sins, and asked Jesus to come into my heart to be my Lord and Savior. Washed by Christ's blood, I felt clean. I was a new man! I knew my rebellion towards God brought much destruction, and my troubles weren't going to disappear overnight. However, I knew Jesus would walk with me every step of the way. Over time, Jesus healed, redeemed, and restored what was broken in my life. Jesus was the champion of my faith. Gently, He continuously encourages me to grow in God's grace and righteousness."

I finished my message by declaring to the congregation, "God's grace and mercy is far greater than your worst sins. If anyone wants prayer come forward now."

An Indonesian man briskly came forward. Despair consumed him. He put his hands on my shoulders, firmly, looked deep into my eyes, and said, "Pastor, do not lie to me. Will the Blood of Jesus wash away all sin, including murder? I must know the truth. Do not lie to me!" Overcome with compassion, I replied, "Yes, it is true. What have you done that has caused you so much guilt and shame?" "I work for one of the richest men in Indonesia. I lead his security team. Basically, we assassinate those who are a threat. I've killed many men," he sadly replied.

With tenderness, I reassured him, "Put your faith and trust in Jesus. Repent of your evil ways and confess your sins, and you will be forgiven. Believe Jesus paid the penalty for all your sins and earnestly follow Him; nothing more is required."

With tears running down his face, he confessed his sins and surrendered his life to Jesus! Like my conversion, God's peace and love flowed into his heart. His countenance swiftly changed from utter anguish to jubilation. He was reborn, and all of Heaven celebrated. I told this man that in God's court, he will never be found guilty of any murder or any other sin; he has been fully forgiven and redeemed for God's glory.

I asked the man what brought him to church that day. He stated that his wife had asked him many times to go, but he always refused. However, something compelled him to go that day. His wife was standing by, listening, and smiling. She knew, and I knew, it was her prayers that brought salvation to her husband.

He was overcome by God's mercy and could not stop declaring God's loving-kindness! He wanted to repay me somehow. With much concern, he stated, "Pastor, the work you and your wife are doing in Indonesia is very, very dangerous. I have accumulated much wealth and have many contacts. I want to offer you protection, free of charge. Whenever you come to Indonesia, I will instruct my security guards to accompany you." With a smile, I replied, "Thank you, but we already have a security team, free of charge." "I don't see them," he replied as he looked around. "Of course, you can't; they are angels sent by God to watch over us as we do His will!"

"For God loved the world so much that He gave His one and only Son, so that everyone who believes in Him will not perish but have eternal life. God sent His Son into the world not to judge the world, but to save the world through Him" (John 3:16-17—NLT).

Reflections

Whenever God opens a door for me to preach, I seek God for wisdom and guidance. There are thousands upon thousands of godly topics to teach. However, God's power is most beautifully expressed when we speak a word in season. God is always intentional and purposeful with His plans. We must never put God into a pattern or method but always seek Him for fresh revelation.

God wanted the Indonesian hitman, who murdered multitudes, to know his identity was not in his sinful nature, but in God's loving grace and mercy.

God met another hitman on the road to Damascus, Saul. Saul, whom Jesus renamed Paul, was a hitman for the religious leaders. Jesus was not deterred by all the people Saul had murdered. Jesus appointed Paul an apostle, prophet, evangelist, pastor, and teacher. Moreover, inspired by the Holy Spirit, Paul wrote 13 Books in the New Testament.

God's mercy is most beautifully seen in those who least deserve it. The Indonesian man, who committed uncountable murders, believed my message about the cleansing power of Jesus' precious Blood. Hence, he found salvation. Like Paul, God has a noble purpose for the Indonesian—beyond anything he could imagine.

I have learned never to judge another by their sins. No matter what they have done, God still loves them. And He desires they know His Son, Jesus. There may be someone in your life who appears to be swallowed by their sinful nature. Seek God to give you a word for those who seemingly have one foot in hell. Perhaps God will use you to snatch them from eternal fire (see Jude 1:23).

A Typhoon and Satanists
Could Not Stop Revival

W̶e received an invite from an Indonesian pastor in Manado, Sulawesi, to be the guest speaker at his church's 50th-anniversary service. We were also asked to conduct numerous open-air and indoor revival/healing services in various cities throughout Sulawesi, one of Indonesia's largest Islands.

The final event would be a two-night healing crusade at an outdoor soccer arena located in Manado. I was informed that I wasn't their first choice - I was their second. Apparently, the first evangelist, who was well known, they invited backed out once he heard that the Church of Satan established their headquarters for Asia in Manado. Supposedly, the Satanists had a reputation for invoking demonic activity. Hearing this, the evangelist became fearful and withdrew from his commitment.

Light belongs in darkness! Greater is He who is in us than who is in the world! God's power is so much more powerful than Satan's; it's laughable. Jesus gives ALL who surrender their lives to Him authority over ALL the power of Satan (see Luke 10:19). Moreover, Jesus stated that ANYONE who believes in Him can do the same works as Him (see John 14:12). Too many Christians needlessly walk in fear because they don't know their identity in Jesus. We were eager to conduct a campaign at the soccer stadium. Moreover, I was expectant God would give grace to the Satanists to hear and believe His Word. We prayed for that!

A team of Filipino missionaries came with us to be our Intercessors and support team. We had met and befriended them in Malaysia. They overflowed with faith, hope, and love, and it was an honor and blessing to have them join us.

Upon arrival, several Indonesian pastors introduced us to Teddy, our Interpreter, for our entire stay. Teddy was a young, vibrant, energetic man who possessed an infectious love for Jesus and people. He's the best Interpreter we have ever had.

One morning we were informed that a powerful typhoon would shortly arrive and cover the entire region with torrential wind and rain. We were designated to conduct an open-air revival/healing meeting that afternoon in a city about a ninety-minute drive from where we were staying. The host pastor informed us that he was canceling the revival meeting due to the typhoon. I passionately objected.

I told the hosting pastor that my team and I would pray for the typhoon to stop. I reminded him that Jesus commanded a storm to stop, and it did. Moreover, Jesus encouraged His doubting disciples they could do the same. Reluctantly, he agreed not to immediately cancel and wait to see if God answered our prayers.

The typhoon raged with no letting up as the day went on. Also, radar showed that the storm would continue to release torrential rain and ferocious wind throughout the evening. Nevertheless, we all kept praying and believing God would perform a miracle. Miracles will never happen when we quit because of what we see with our carnal vision. We must persevere in faith and prayers, always keeping our sight on Jesus.

The typhoon had not relented when it was time to depart for the revival meeting. Nevertheless, not focusing on the dire circumstances, we kept our eyes firmly on Jesus, and we all climbed into a van. It was a slow drive; rain pounded our van; visibility was poor; the wind howled, and our van continuously swayed. Nevertheless, we kept praying and believing for a miracle the entire way.

Just as we were pulling into a beautiful city park designated for our campaign, the heavens opened, and the sun shone through. Mysteriously, the opening in the clouds was only above where we would be conducting our meeting. Everywhere else, the typhoon carried on. It was an unbelievable miracle.

We arrived a couple of hours before our meeting started, allowing our host and his team to set up the stage and sound equipment.

I asked Kathy to preach that night. I knew God would move with His power; Kathy always preaches from Heavenly Father's heart. After Kathy's sermon, she gave an altar call, and multitudes came forward to receive a loving touch from God. We have many testimonies from that evening, but I will share just two that especially touched my heart.

A family came with an elderly man, who appeared to be the grandfather. As they walked from the parking lot, a young man, possibly a grandson, carried a chair for his grandfather. As they made their way forward to the front, the entire family would stop every few feet for the elderly man to sit and rest. After quite some time, they finally made it to the front, allowing the elderly man to sit and relax throughout the event. That is the type of desperate hunger God cannot resist!

Kathy watched this family proceed the entire way from the parking lot to the very front. After giving an altar call and being moved by their faith, Kathy immediately went to this family and asked them if they wanted prayers. The elderly man who was partially crippled asked Kathy to pray healing for his legs. What happened next was both endearing and humorous.

Immediately after receiving Kathy's prayers, the elderly man stood up from his chair, turned around, and ran off like a twenty-year-old in a race. Amazed, his family picked up his chair and ran after him, laughing and rejoicing! It was one of the strangest healings we have ever encountered.

A mother with several children came to me for prayer. I asked her how I could pray. She responded, "I have many children, and I am destitute. Recently, I became pregnant with another child. I can barely take care of the children I have, so I decided to have an abortion. I am not a Christian, but after hearing the message tonight, I know Jesus can and will help me through my troubles. I have decided not to have an abortion. Would you pray for me to receive Jesus as my Lord and Savior?" Tears flowed down her cheeks and mine as we prayed and celebrated her new birth in Jesus. It was a marvelous sight to see her gently rub her womb and cherish her unborn child.

Amazingly, right after our crusade ended and after the crew packed away all the equipment, the clouds closed above us, and the torrential rain returned. We were in awe of God. We praised God and rejoiced all the way back to our lodging.

God continued to visit all our campaigns with power and miracles. Our two-night revival meeting in Manado's soccer stadium was no exception.

I was informed that many Satanists were planning to attend our event to invoke curses on our team and us. God had different plans for them. God possessed the same unfathomable love for them as anyone else despite their rebellion.

As I mentioned, Teddy was a brilliant Interpreter. God gave Teddy grace to interpret every nuance of my message clearly, and with the same enthusiasm.

On the first night, I warned the Satanists of God's judgment if they did not repent of their sins and turn to God. God made it very clear to me to inform them their window for repentance was short. I told them their curses held no power over us because blessings are more powerful than curses and that we had prayed for God to pour out His blessings on their lives. I shared God loves them deeply, and so do we.

God opened the hearts of several Satanists; they came forward and surrendered their lives to Jesus. I also had a powerful message for the Muslims who attended the event.

Surprisingly, the hosting pastors, about six of them, were not happy with my message. The next evening, before I preached, all the pastors gathered to lecture me. Fearful of my rebuke, one pastor timidly spoke, "Pastor Mark, we are concerned about your boldness. Indonesia is a Muslim country, and an influential Muslim owns this stadium. We are fearful that your preaching is going to get us into trouble with the owner and the Muslim authorities."

I was annoyed by their lack of faith. In their presence, I turned to Teddy, my Interpreter, and said, "Pray with me that God will give us a double measure of boldness for tonight. Pray with me that God lights us on fire for all to see. We prayed, and Teddy informed the pastors of what I shared. They didn't respond but departed with forlorn faces.

Both Teddy and I knew God answered our prayers; that evening we burned with God's holy fire! I preached with greater boldness and authority than the night before. And God showed up with incredible power. The next day we were scheduled to return to Malaysia. But before we did, we gathered with the pastors for breakfast. Again, the pastors wanted to share their hearts with me.

One of them said, "Pastor Mark, we apologize for our lack of faith and ask for your forgiveness. After you gave your message last night, the Muslim owner of the arena approached us. He was deeply touched by your message. He especially loved hearing how much Jesus loves Muslims. In fact, he was so moved by your sermon, he forgave our rental debt for using his arena."

Choked with emotion, I told the pastors there was nothing to forgive. We were honored to serve alongside them in their beautiful country.

By my power I will make my people strong, and by my authority they will go wherever they wish. I, the LORD, have spoken,"
(Zechariah 10:12 - NLT)!

Reflections

Satan will always strive to stop God's kingdom from advancing. It's called "spiritual warfare" (see Ephesians 6:10-20). However, if we engage in spiritual warfare with godly weapons, it's not even a fair contest; we will defeat the devil at every turn. Jesus secured ALL our victories on the "Cross at Calvary." However, we must persevere in battle until we secure victory.

Our godly weapons are not worldly, but they possess divine power to destroy the works of the devil (see 2 Corinthians 10:4). Prayer, faith, an intimate relationship with Jesus, godly authority, truth, peace, and unconditional love are some of our weapons. When appropriately used, these weapons will destroy every satanic attack.

Satan wanted to prevent Jesus and His disciples from crossing the lake, so he stirred up a powerful storm. Frightened, the disciples woke Jesus. Jesus rebuked the storm then admonished His disciples for their lack of faith. Jesus clearly states that we can do the same works as Him (see John 14:12). Believing Jesus, we rebuked the typhoon in Indonesia. As a result, multitudes found healing and salvation.

Moreover, Satan sent his disciples to ruin our revival meetings. However, we engaged in battle with divine weapons to destroy their plans. Satan has no answer to love, and blessings are infinitely more powerful than curses. Consequently, some Satanists were reborn and became God's precious children.

Don't lose heart if you are in the middle of a spiritual battle and feeling overwhelmed. Jesus is always with you; set your gaze on Him, and victory will be yours. Behold His majesty and continuously strengthen yourself in His Spirit. Learn how to use your spiritual weapons and never give up in the battle. Always remember Jesus secured your victory on the Cross. Patiently endure until you receive the glory of your hope (see James 1:12). God loves you deeply and wants you to succeed!

Diabetic Muslim Man is Miraculously Healed

While we lived in Malaysia, I would arise early for morning walks. Those moments were a magnificent and intimate time with God. I relished being alone with Jesus. I sang, prayed, and sought wisdom from above and enjoyed the sunrise as I walked through my neighborhood.

Malaysian mornings are gloriously beautiful and pleasantly warm. A variety of exotic flowers, plants, and bushes adorn the landscape. And tropical birds continuously sing as if they were conducting a symphony. I dearly miss those times. Our mission work in S.E. Asia was perilous; we faced fresh challenges daily. My morning walks were essential to receive wisdom, encouragement, and guidance.

One particular morning, as I was walking through our neighborhood, Jesus gave me an unusual request, "Mark, go across the street to the next neighborhood. I want to show you something." Trusting I heard from God, I crossed the road, climbed over a fence, and carefully proceeded down a muddy hill into an impoverished neighborhood known as Bukit Ikhlas.

I then asked Jesus, "What would you have me do now." Jesus replied, "Prophesy over the neighborhood, and bless the residents in my name." And so, I did. I walked the streets, and when I had the unction of the Holy Spirit, I prophesied. Being a white person, I was a strange sight for the residents. However, I had become accustomed to people staring at me and used those awkward moments as opportunities to share Jesus.

On the way back to my house, Jesus instructed me to return to Bukit Ikhlas the next day. He said I would find the mayor of Bukit Ikhlas at a restaurant, and when I did, to bless him. The next day, Kathy, I, and one of our spiritual sons went there to find the mayor.

We saw a restaurant that appeared to serve delicious food when we arrived. So, we chose that establishment to hopefully meet the mayor. After we were seated at a table, we asked our server if he knew the mayor and if he was there. He knew him but informed us he was not present. After waiting for an hour or so, the mayor never showed. So, we left. Our meal was tasty, though.

On the way back to our house, I asked Jesus, "Why didn't we find the mayor?" Jesus graciously replied, "You went to the wrong restaurant. But do not worry, you will find the mayor at the restaurant directly across the street from the one you were at. Go tomorrow, and you will find him there." Sure enough, we met the mayor the next day at a restaurant, directly across the street from the one the day before, just as Jesus stated. In hindsight, I should have asked Jesus which restaurant the mayor would be at and not assumed.

After inquiring our server if he knew the mayor and where he might be, he graciously took us to the mayor's table and introduced us. After our greetings, I shared with the mayor (Mohamed) how my God led us to meet him at the restaurant, not leaving out any details. Also, we discovered Mohamed was more than a mayor; this man was a representative of the UMNO political party, a hardcore Muslim party known to hate and persecute Christians.

Introducing Jesus to the mayor would be an awkward and delicate endeavor. I'm so grateful to Heavenly Father for sending the Holy Spirit who gives us boldness, wisdom, discernment, and power. I needed all that and more for this encounter with the mayor.

Not deterred by intimidation, I informed Mohamed that we were Christians. I emphasized Lord Jesus sent us to bless him and his community. Thankfully, Mohamed responded graciously. He was kind and gentle and gave us no opposition. After sharing the Good News and some testimonies of God's goodness, I asked Mohamed if he knew anyone who was sick whom we could pray for. Inspired by our witness, he told us that one of his best friends was afflicted by severe diabetes. He inquired, "If you are willing to pray for my friend (Jafaar), I will take you to his apartment now." Obviously, Mohamed loved his friend and was willing to risk his reputation and career in hopes our God would heal him.

It was a surreal moment observing a Muslim leader from a hardcore political party that strongly opposed Christianity allow us into his community to reveal Jesus. It did not matter that we believed in a different God than him; his love for his friend compelled him to set aside his beliefs in hopes that Jesus would heal his good friend. We enthusiastically agreed to go. Mohamed led us to a dilapidated, congested apartment complex, where Jafaar lived with his wife and six children. Their apartment was small, cluttered, and crowded. We found the family to be friendly and welcoming, though.

After introductions, Jafaar shared that he went to a clinic three times a week for kidney dialysis treatment. And that his health was progressively getting worse. We shared the gospel of salvation and some healing testimonies done in Jesus' Name. Encouraged by our words, Jafaar welcomed our prayers for healing. We placed our hands on this kind man and asked Jesus to give him a supernatural blood transfusion. It was evident that Jafaar was moved by God's presence.

We returned one week later to see if Jafaar had been healed; he was not. It did not matter; Jafaar and his family enjoyed our company and encouraged us to come and pray anytime. However, it was apparent their oldest son was not happy with our presence. Later, we were informed he was a member of a Muslim mafia organization.

Over the next few months, we continued to visit this family and pray that Jesus would give our new friend a miraculous blood transfusion. Though God had not healed Jafaar after several prayer sessions, our love for one another grew deeper and deeper. Also, Jafaar and his wife welcomed our biblical stories. Though they were unwilling to convert to Christianity, they were inspired and encouraged by Christ's teachings and the gospels. Moreover, we continued to make more and more friends in Bukit Ikhlas, a predominately Muslim neighborhood. God was moving in this community despite our friend not being healed.

Then came the glorious report! After several months of receiving prayer, Jafaar shared that Jesus had answered our prayers and totally healed him of diabetes. With tears, we rejoiced with him and his family.

I asked Jafaar how he knew for sure that he was healed. He answered with an extraordinary testimony. With a broad smile, Jafaar delightfully expressed, "On my last visit, my doctor administered blood tests and was dumbfounded by the results. Shocked, my doctor inquired, 'Where have you been going for diabetes treatment? Your blood is 100% clean.' I responded I have been going nowhere except here. In disbelief and with much anger, my doctor snapped, 'You are lying; nobody gets healed from diabetes; I must know about this new treatment.' My doctor was furious with me. With trepidation, I told him an American Christian couple prayed for me. God heard their prayers and healed me. My doctor refused to believe me and was furious!"

Shortly later, Jafaar and his wife surrendered their lives to Jesus. We became part of their family structure and celebrated many special occasions, including weddings and holidays. Also, we bought a motorbike for Jafaar to find work.

When the mayor of Bukit Ikhlas, Mohamed, heard about Jesus' healing Jaffar, he was struck with awe and conviction. Beautifully, Mohamed surrendered his life to Jesus, as well. However, overcome with fear, Mohamed pleaded, "Don't tell anyone of my conversion. If my political party discovers I've converted to Christianity, they will murder me."

Understandably, that is a typical response for Muslims who convert to Christianity. However, we have seen in many converts that as God perfects His love in their hearts, their fear melts away over time! Moreover, as God's ambassadors of love, it is our responsibility to teach our disciples how to grow in God's grace and love. And what a joy, honor, and privilege that is.

As I mentioned, their oldest son had joined a highly organized Muslim mafia, which brought much distress to his parents. Their son is a strong, intelligent, charming, and confident young man who needs to be the rooster in his family. Our presence made him uncomfortable. He could have easily had us hurt or assassinated, but he liked us. He admired our boldness, faith, and purity. Also, he knew our prayers carried supernatural power, which brought him a measure of fear of our God.

Wanting to put me in my place, he attempted to intimidate me. He looked intently into my eyes and warned me, "Mark, I know you and Kathy have power, but I have greater power than you." I knew that was a threat; we had become accustomed to them. I didn't flinch; I never do. Jesus is always with us and gives us the grace to be bold and stand firm in our faith in those situations!

Diverting his threat, I responded with a smile and acknowledged our fondness for him. Our conversation ended with this young man giving me an approving smile and hug. He knew we loved him and that his threats would not intimidate us. With affection, he accepted and welcomed us into his family!

On an early morning prayer walk, Jesus spoke, I obeyed, and salvation came to many! Love will always find a way!

Jesus traveled throughout the region of Galilee, teaching in the synagogues and announcing the Good News about the Kingdom. And he healed every kind of disease and illness, (Matthew 4:23 - NLT).

Reflections

God's Word states that He will pour out His Spirit on ALL Believers, and they will prophesy and shall have dreams and visions (see Acts 2:17). Dreams and visions are powerful ways God speaks to His children. In the Old Testament, only a select few were blessed by this divine occurrence. Now, it is for all those who believe in Jesus.

God instructed me to go alone and release a prophetic word over a Muslim village (Bukit Ikhlas). Also, God gave me a vision of what He wanted to accomplish. I complied, walked the streets of Bukit Ikhlas, and audibly released God's blessings. God was faithful to watch over and perform His Word; it did not come back void but fulfilled its purpose. Consequently, a diabetic Muslim man received miraculous healing, and he, his household, and the mayor found salvation. Moreover, God planted revival seeds in Bukit Ikhlas. Only when we arrive in Heaven will we see the fullness of our obedience.

Pay attention to your dreams and visions. Not all dreams are from God, but those from Him have a mighty purpose for His will in your life. Seek God for clarity and understanding when you have a dream or vision that moves your spirit. If you are uncertain of the meaning, seek someone who has the gift to interpret dreams. And remember, wisdom from God is always pure, gentle, full of mercy and goodness, and sincere (see James 3:17).

Blowing a Shofar in a Muslim Village Leads to Revival

We had been evangelizing in Muslim villages all morning. As we traveled to another, I felt prompted to stop and eat at a particular restaurant. There was nothing unusual about that, but God had a special assignment He desired to reveal at that establishment.

I noticed a newsstand just inside the entrance of the restaurant. I rarely read Malaysian newspapers, but I was prompted to look at the front-page headlines. The article was about a recent monsoon storm that caused catastrophic flooding in Pembuang. A primary river had overflowed, submerging the entire village, which rested on its banks. Consequently, all the villagers were relocated to a community center until the waters receded.

Jesus instructed me to bring resources, comfort, and the Gospel to Pembuang. Later, I discovered this village promoted radical Islamic ideology—they were known as a village that sympathized with Islamic terrorists. We were informed by other Muslims we would be killed if we tried to evangelize the residents. However, Jesus loves those people and had a plan for their salvation! We were honored that God had chosen us to be His 'carriers' of compassion and redemption.

As I have mentioned, once God commands us to go somewhere, we refuse to take a risk assessment to determine plausibility. We just believe and obey. Of course, we wrestle with fear when we receive dangerous mission assignments. However, God's love perfected in our hearts always melts away our worries. To receive His amazing love, we spend much time in worship and prayer until we are overcome by God's Spirit. And where the Spirit of the Lord is, there is freedom from fear. Moreover, in those precious encounters, God impregnates us with faith to move mountains.

We never assume God's plans, nor make them a method by repeating what God has instructed in the past. However, we always adhere to evangelical biblical principles and seek the Holy Spirit on their expression for each new assignment.

I asked Jesus, "What would you have us do in Pembuang." Jesus replied, "Buy a shofar (ram's horn) and learn how to blow it. Once you arrive in Pembuang, I will show you where to stop. A crowd will gather to investigate your intentions. Tell them I sent you to bless their village. Also, tell the gathering I instructed you to blow a shofar which will signal my angels to come and heal the sick in their village." We believed Jesus spoke and committed ourselves to obey, even though it sounded crazy.

It took two months before I found a place in Malaysia that made shofars. With some effort, I learned how to blow the shofar well.

One month later, after the waters had receded and the Pembuang villagers had returned to their homes, we made the eight-hour journey to their village.

Once there, we slowly drove down the main street seeking God's prompting where to stop. God guided us to park by a grocery store in the middle of the town. After getting out of our car, God directed me to a specific spot to stand and address the residents present. I will share later the significance of that exact location. It had powerful spiritual implications.

White people never come to this village. So, it did not take much time for a crowd to gather and investigate our motives. As I faced the gathering, I was overcome by God's love for all present. The unction of the Holy Spirit welled up inside me, compelling me to speak with bold faith. Overcome with joy, I expressed how much Jesus and Heavenly Father loved them and wanted to bless and heal them. And with much zeal and compassion, I proclaimed the Good News of Salvation.

I told the crowd that Jesus had instructed me to blow the shofar I was holding. And when I did, that would signal angels to come and heal the sick in their village. The crowd intently listened and appeared curious by my words.

I could see they were love-starved and dwelled in much hopelessness. Rigid religion had not brought the residents peace or happiness. They were sheep without a shepherd wandering in confusion. Though my message of salvation was a strange doctrine to them, they were moved by the beauty of my words.

When it was time to blow the shofar, I was apprehensive; my lips refused to cooperate. I would be lying if I said that I never wrestle with fear and doubt. God asked us to do a bizarre prophetic act in a diehard Muslim village. I thought to myself, "Did God really speak to me? Am I crazy!"

When I blew the shofar, a squeaky sound went forth. The crowd stood perplexed. With an uneasy smile, I expressed that I was nervous, which caused my lips to tense, and I would attempt to blow the shofar again. I did, and the same ghastly sound pierced the atmosphere. They were not impressed. Yet, they remained curious about what would happen next.

I looked up into the heavens, hoping to hear from God, and He did not disappoint. After receiving an encouraging word from my Lord, I set my gaze on the crowd and confidently proclaimed, "My God is pleased with my effort; His angels are on their way to bring healing for those who are sick. Is there anyone here who would like to receive prayer?"

God understands our weaknesses. It's our faithful obedience that moves His spirit, not the excellence of our performance. We should be more concerned about the quality of love we demonstrate than the quality of our presentation.

God gave us immense favor, and we prayed for many sick people that day, sharing the Good News of Salvation with them all.

Before we started praying for people, a man came forward and asked me why I chose to stand and speak from that spot. I responded, "My God told me to stand there; why do you ask?"

Bewildered, he shared an extraordinary story. One year earlier, an African witch doctor visited their village and stood in the exact spot. He killed an animal, poured its blood on the ground, and invoked a curse over Pembuang. Then the African witch doctor cursed Pembuang with disease and illness. After he summoned a curse, the witch doctor swiftly left, never to be seen or heard from again.

Wow, the witch doctor poured out blood and cursed the village from the very spot I preached the Good News, performed a prophetic act, and declared a blessing. God wanted to demonstrate to Pembuang His blessings are far greater than demonic curses.

Witchcraft has always been a large part of Malaysian culture. The witch doctors were skilled at invoking spiritual activity. In fact, mysteriously, many people became sick and demonically tormented by their curses.

However, in God's unfathomable mercy, He chose us to break the curse from that exact spot the witch doctor had killed an animal and poured out its blood. The villagers were astounded by that event.

When we visited this village a short time later, the Holy Spirit prompted me to meet the village Imam (Muslim priest). As I mentioned, he promoted terroristic ideology. A resident we befriended led us to the Imam's house.

I was very straightforward with the Imam. I informed him that we were Christians, and our God instructed us to bless his village. The Imam listened carefully. I could see in his demeanor that he was not angry. I'm sure the testimonies of our earlier visit reached him. I then asked him for his blessing to continue to serve his village. I didn't need the Imam's approval to do God's work. But for some mysterious reason, God wanted me to seek his blessing.

The village Imam not only gave his blessing, but he also thanked us for our kindness. The Imam expressed we had good hearts and were generous people. Moreover, he said we could come and serve his village anytime. AMAZING FAVOR! When a man's ways please God, He will make even his enemies be at peace with him (see Proverbs 16:7).

Not everyone in that village appreciated our presence though, some wanted to kill us, including the resident witch doctor; He became jealous of our power and popularity. However, we won the hearts of multitudes, including a Muslim woman (Amira) who led us to the homes of those who were sick or demonically tormented.

On our second trip to this village, Amira led us to a house whose father had endured excruciating pain for fourteen years. He had a severe case of gout and suffered from skin disease and heart ailments. When we arrived, this father, Amir, was lying on his bed, weeping loudly. He had been bedridden for six months, with no hope for relief. His miserable condition struck us to the core; our hearts ached for God to heal him. This humble man begged for us to pray for his healing! Day and night, Amir endured unbearable agony. His neighbors could hear his wailing every night.

I lived with severe chronic pain for five years before receiving miraculous healing. Kathy's prayers and faith healed me. That experience has given me unusual compassion for others experiencing the same. Also, it was the seed that brought Kathy and me into the healing ministry.

We placed our hands on Amir and prayed for healing. Miraculously, Jesus immediately healed this Muslim of all his afflictions. It was an amazing and glorious moment. Amir's wife and children cried with joy and praised God! Convicted by God's mercy, kindness, and power, Amir, his wife, and mother-in-law surrendered their lives to Jesus. I have an adorable video of Amir and his family testifying his and his mother-in-law's healing.

Whenever we visited Amir and his family, neighbors would come, uninvited, to receive prayers. There is conviction and hope in the testimony of God's goodness!

Later, we helped Amir establish two small businesses. However, persecution stood at Amir's door. Succumbed by threats, Amir returned to the Islam faith. Sadly, several years later, he mysteriously died. However, we continued to disciple his family for many years. I believe Jesus granted Amir an opportunity to repent and return to Him before he died. Amir always remained an honorable man and good friend.

On another visit to Pembuang, we were informed a group of residents was waiting for us upon our arrival. They had gathered at a house and instructed a resident, Amira, who became a friend, to bring us to their home. Testimonies of what God was doing through us spread throughout their village and the surrounding region, encouraging some Muslims to seek us who were hungry for a divine touch.

Amira led us to a dozen Muslims sitting on a front porch waiting for our arrival. After introductions, I immediately started to share the Gospel of Salvation. Alarmed by my message, a woman abruptly stood and screamed, "You are Christians and trying to convert us. I'm going to report you to the religious police." She screamed threats nonstop as she ran to her house, which was nearby. In fact, she continued yelling insults and threats from her window.

My mission team wanted to leave immediately. Understandably, they were frightened by her threats. Seeking God for wisdom and discernment, the Holy Spirit assured me her threats were empty, and she would not report us. Besides, compassion gripped Kathy and me as we saw the faces of those waiting to hear about our God and receive prayer. They were hungry and desperate souls, and we would not deny them a divine encounter with Jesus. Most likely, they would never have another opportunity. It ended well; the angry woman did not report us, and everyone was blessed by our message and prayers.

Compelled to read the morning headlines from a newspaper brought salvation to some Muslims residing in a hardcore Islamic village. Many others now have a favorable opinion of Christianity. Moreover, multitudes of kingdom seeds were planted in countless hearts. We have numerous other beautiful testimonies from this village. Perhaps I will write about those in another book.

"When you hear the priests give one long blast on the rams' horns, have all the people shout as loud as they can. Then the walls of the town will collapse, and the people can charge straight into the town,"
(*Joshua 6:5 - NLT*).

Reflections

Prophetic acts are mentioned in both the Old and New Testaments. Whenever God instructed His children to perform a prophetic act, it released a powerful manifestation of His glory. Remember what happened at Jericho? The walls came down because of a prophetic act.And when Moses stretched his hand towards the sea, God separated the waters, making way for the Israelites deliverance. And there are countless other prophetic acts mentioned in the Bible.

Blowing the shofar in a radical Islamic village was only one of many prophetic acts God instructed us to perform in S.E. Asia. Every one of those acts released an unusual occurrence of God's glory. I will be writing about these prophetic acts in another book.

When I blew the shofar in Pembuang, several things happened. God's light pierced the dominion of darkness over Pembuang; angels descended to assist us in our ministry; several residents received healings, deliverances, and salvation; and the village Imam blessed our mission work. Moreover, kingdom seeds were planted in multitudes.

You may have had an impression to say or do something that made no sense. Pay attention to those impressions and seek God for revelation, wisdom, and guidance. He may be asking you to release His glory in your family, community, or a special event. If your highest motive is loving God and others, don't worry about making mistakes. Jesus is Lord of your missteps and will gently bring understanding and correction. He will even use your blunders for His glory. Seek and grow in the gift of prophecy. If you do so, you will have no regrets. God desires to use you for his noble purposes.

Confronting a Poltergeist Spirit in a Muslim Haunted House

Malaysia's premier newspaper, the Malaysian Star, featured an article about a poltergeist spirit wreaking havoc in a house located in Lampung, a hard-core Islamic village. The testimonies about this demonic presence were so fantastical they reached the surrounding countries prompting a constant stream of media reporters to investigate. Moreover, renowned witch doctors and spiritists from Malaysia and other countries came to the possessed house, hoping to cast out the demon to showcase their power and gain glory.

Apparently, the poltergeist spirit was lighting small fires everywhere in the house, unexpectedly and frequently, in plain sight of those present. Mysteriously, flames would suddenly appear on non-flammable and flammable objects including, clothing, cement tile, appliances, and tile walls. The Malaysian Star reported that one of their reporters counted eighty fire outbreaks in one day.

We had a particular interest in this story because it happened in a Muslim village we were currently serving, Lampung. On our next visit to Lampung, we decided to investigate this bizarre story. Could this be a showdown of God's power vs. the power of darkness? If so, it would not be a legitimate contest. Much greater is God's power than Satan's; it's not even a worthy discussion. Moreover, Jesus has given us authority over ALL the power of Satan (see Luke 10:19).

It was an eight-hour drive to Lampung. Once we arrived, we went straightaway to a friend's residence and asked him to bring us to the possessed house. We arrived after sunset, so we had to walk several blocks in darkness and torrential rain. It was monsoon season. When we arrived at the house, it was packed with people. Many locals who could not enter the house stood outside, willingly getting soaked, not wanting to miss a big moment.

The owner, an elderly Muslim woman (Inayah), who knew our friend, allowed inside. Inayah, her daughter-in-law, and two granddaughters lived in this possessed house.

As we entered the house, everyone inside shouted to be heard because the rain relentlessly pounded the tin roof - it was deafening. The scene was beyond surreal. Fear and uncertainty consumed the atmosphere; the mood was depressingly gloomy.

Muslim priests trained in exorcism were discussing how to cast out the demon. They appeared to be consumed with fear. For over two weeks, exorcists and spiritists had failed to expel the poltergeist spirit, so they doubted the success of their methods.

A senior reporter for the Islamic newspaper, the Harakah Daily, investigated the strange occurrences. His wife was busy taking pictures of burnt items and fires as they broke out. Amid all this commotion, Inayah, her daughter-in-law, and two granddaughters cowered in a corner.

It wasn't long after our arrival before everyone in the room glared at us. I knew what they were thinking, "What is the white couple doing here?" We stuck out like flashing neon lights. We felt their contempt! Nevertheless, that was typical of our life in Malaysia, and we had become accustomed to those awkward moments.

Noticing the senior reporter spoke excellent English, I asked him where he learned it. He told me he received a master's degree in journalism from a college in England. His countenance showed he wasn't pleased with our presence. With a condescending tone, he asked, "Why are you here?" Boldly, I responded, "I am a Christian pastor, and in the Name of Jesus, I can command the evil spirit to leave, and it will. Jesus has given me the authority to do so." He was visibly annoyed by my proclamation.

I asked the reporter who all the people were in the house. He replied, "A few men are Imams trained in exorcism; the others are witch doctors and spiritists." I responded, "They appear to be frightened and not having any success. If I am allowed, I will command the evil to leave, and it will, instantly." My boldness in Jesus sometimes is perceived as arrogance. I sensed my statement irritated the reporter. He told me to wait where I was standing. He then gathered the men in the house to discuss my proposal.

One of our spiritual sons overheard their discussion and said to me, "We are in big trouble; you really ticked off the reporter. He thinks you are full of pride." I responded, "Relax, when confronting evil, Satan will always attempt to bring us under the dominion of fear. And if we don't resist, our faith will be severely hindered." I must admit, though, it was a tenuous situation that could have gone badly.

When the reporter returned, he asked me, "Okay, pastor, how would you cast out the evil spirit?" "I want to share with all present how I would do so. Bring everyone together and have them sit on the floor," I responded.

He complied and instructed everyone to sit and hear about the white man's exorcism plan. They appeared anxious but also curious. For weeks, their exorcism efforts had failed. God had a broader purpose than teaching them how I would expel the evil spirit, though. Through bizarre circumstances, God had gathered a captive audience to hear about Jesus and His plan for salvation. Some men were Islamic clerics from various communities, which was significant. Sitting right in front of me was a fantastic opportunity to plant eternal seeds and glorify God. I pray for these opportunities. I had no trepidation; God had given me boldness, and I knew I had His unmerited favor.

With conviction and compassion, I shared Jesus and His Crucifixion! I also shared how Jesus saved me from many horrible sins and delivered me from the kingdom of darkness to the kingdom of light. I spoke clearly about God's transforming power through a relationship with Jesus.

God opened their eyes and hearts to give serious reflection to my testimony. However, they remained frightened. Everyone listening sat motionless, looking straight at me, not wanting anyone in the room to see their conviction and reverence, for fear of persecution. Nevertheless, God profoundly touched them through my testimonies and presentation of Christ's Gospel. I know God's angels were present, ministering to those whom God removed the veil of deception (see Hebrews 1:14).

But when one turns to the Lord, the veil is removed
(2 Corinthians 3:16 - ESV).

And even if our gospel is veiled, it is veiled to those who are perishing. In their case the god of this world has blinded the minds of the unbelievers, to keep them from seeing the light of the gospel of the glory of Christ, who is the image of God (2 Corinthians 4:3-4 - ESV).

As I preached, others were listening through the windows and front door. Inayah, her daughter-in-law, and two granddaughters found a place of refuge, hiding behind Kathy. Kathy walks with an extraordinary measure of divine peace, so it never surprises me when others want to be in her company, even if they don't know her. It warmed my heart that this family felt safe in Kathy's presence (see Isaiah 60:1-3).

However, I perceived Inayah was filled with pride and rebellion. She was soaking up all the attention, and most likely, making a nice profit by allowing the evil spirit to manifest in her house.She was destitute and welcomed the numerous donations from the constant stream of visitors. Moreover, our friend who lived nearby told us that the elderly women enjoyed and practiced witchcraft.Consequently, unless Inayah repented, the demon would only return if cast out!

When I finished preaching, the Harakah Daily reporter asked me to step aside where he could talk to me privately. Fearfully, he pleaded, "Pastor, please do not cast out the evil spirit."

God revealed to me why the senior reporter was panicky. He reported for Malaysia's premier Islamic newspaper. He knew if he published a story about a Christian casting out a demon after multitudes of Muslim exorcists and witch doctors could not, he would be persecuted by his Muslim community and authorities. The reporter believed my testimony about Jesus Christ. Also, he knew God had given me the power to cleanse the house of evil. Sadly, he chose to be a coward rather than courageous.

I asked God what He wanted me to do. He told me that if I cast out the demon, the evil spirit would return with other more powerful demons as soon as we left (see Matthew 12:43-45).The elderly woman loved witchcraft and would welcome them back. God told me to let the woman reap the desires of her heart. She heard the Gospel, but God hardened her heart because she refused to repent.

Believing God, I agreed not to cast out the demon. But before we left, I declared a prophetic word over the senior reporter. I prophesized, "Presently, you are a reporter for Harakah Daily, but my God is going to relentlessly pursue you. In the future, you will be a reporter for Jesus Christ." He was terrified by my words and abruptly excused himself without responding.

Not long after, we were informed the possessed house burned down! We weren't surprised.

One year later, while I was in a government building in that same region, I noticed the same reporter from the Harakah Daily. He was standing a short distance down a hallway. I yelled at him, "Remember me?" He looked my way, noticed who I was, and literally ran in the other direction. It's interesting because he could easily have had me arrested. However, I believe the fear of my God prevented him from doing so.

When a man's ways please the Lord, he makes even his enemies be at peace with him (Proverbs 16:7).

It was sad that the elderly Muslim woman would not repent. It was doubly distressing to see her family suffer because of her love for evil and rebellion towards God. However, I believe God used us to plant kingdom seeds in all those present on that dreary, rainy night. Moreover, I am convinced God will pursue that Islamic reporter until he surrenders his life to Jesus Christ. I can't be positive, but I think he believed my message about Jesus to be the truth, and as a result, he's wrestling with God.

"My thoughts are nothing like your thoughts," says the LORD. "And my ways are far beyond anything you could imagine. For just as the heavens are higher than the earth, so my ways are higher than your ways and my thoughts higher than your thoughts"
(Isaiah 55:8-9 - NLT).

Reflections

Jesus gave power and authority to his disciples over demons and diseases (see Luke 9:1-2). Moreover, he gave his disciples authority over ALL the power of evil (see Luke 10:19). Sadly, too many Christians are ignorant of God's Word; consequently, they needlessly suffer from demonic attacks. Jesus asked a profound question to His disciples, "Will I find faith when I return to earth" (see Luke 18:8)?

We will always have trials and troubles for following Jesus. However, it is possible to possess peace, joy, and hope amid our worst crises. Genuine and sincere faith in Jesus—who is God's Living Word—is our answer for all our troubles. God's Word must be alive and active in our lives to destroy Satan's plans. Jesus restored many broken relationships in my life. Healed me from three incurable infirmities. And delivered me from several bondages.

Moreover, Jesus vanquished debilitating depression from my life. In replacement, Jesus blessed me with divine peace that transcends human understanding. And, beautifully, heavenly joy constantly renews my strength.

Kathy and I have had countless confrontations on the mission field with witch doctors, satanists, demon-possessed, and others who meant us harm. Jesus, in us, destroyed their efforts at every corner. I am grateful we learned about spiritual warfare in our own community before God sent us to S.E. Asia. They were invaluable lessons!

In Jesus, you are the "Victor," not a victim! You are the "Head," not the tail! You are above and not beneath! Though the enemy comes against you in one direction, he will flee from you in seven (see Deuteronomy 28:7)! Don't give the devil an inch. You put him under your feet! Can I hear an "AMEN?"

Motorcycle Accident Opens
Doors for Evangelism

While we lived in Malaysia, we resided in the Kuala Lumpur metropolitan area, populated by seven million people. Soon after moving to Malaysia, we bought a secondhand car. Sadly, we quickly discovered getting around in this bustling city was not the same as in Minnesota. The highways were continuously jammed with vehicles moving at a snail's pace. Hence, it took an enormous amount of time to get anywhere.

However, I noticed the motorcyclists would zip through and around all the cars. Though I was informed motorcycle deaths in Malaysia were a significant cause of fatalities, it didn't matter. I could accomplish much more with a motorcycle. So, I decided to buy a 125cc Honda. In my late teen years, I owned a motorbike. I missed the thrills of those experiences and relished the opportunity for more.

I was excited about my purchase, and it wasn't long before I was moving as quickly as all the other motorcyclists. That purchase opened many new doors. Before sunrise, I would hop on my motorbike and proceed to a nearby beautiful Park. That Park was my sanctuary. As I walked its trails through beautiful, forested terrain, I prayed and worshipped. It was my favorite part of the day.

Also, Kathy and I used my motorbike to visit remote villages in the jungle with our team. Many of these villages were only accessible by motorbike. It was an unbelievable honor and joy to bring the Good News of Salvation to these remote tribes. My motorbike served us well until one eventful day. But even then, God changed misery into victory.

I was in a hurry and driving recklessly to reach an appointment. Unfortunately, my carelessness caused an accident. Another driver, no fault of his own, hit me with his SUV. I flew off my motorbike and tumbled onto the hard pavement. Lying in the middle of the road with a broken shoulder, I could not move. The driver who hit me paused, looked at me with pity, then drove off. All the other drivers did the same; they cautiously maneuvered around me and continued their journey without stopping to help. I was in excruciating pain and irritated by their lack of compassion.

Not wanting to be run over and wincing in pain, I crawled to my motorbike and forced myself to stand and get back on. Gratefully, it started and was drivable—though barely. I drove home carefully, groaning the whole way.

Once I arrived home, I yelled for Kathy to come and assist me. My whole body ached, and the pain in my shoulder was unbearable. Kathy rushed me to the nearest hospital with three of our spiritual sons. Once we arrived, they fetched a wheelchair and brought me to the waiting room.

A young man and four police officers sat nearby. The young man was handcuffed to one of the officers who were Muslim. Compelled by compassion, I decided to push my agony aside to engage with the young man who appeared consumed in despair. Empathy is a beautiful gift from God that often leads to evangelical encounters.

Tenderly, I said, "Young man, do you speak English." He nodded, acknowledging that he did. I commented, "You must have done something very, very bad to be sitting with four policemen and handcuffed to one." The young man wasn't offended by my observation - shame, terror, and hopelessness consumed him. He sat silent, guilt-ridden, with no response.

Wanting to bring hope, I said, "I have been in your very spot because of the bad choices I made. I know how you are feeling. I have spent much time in jail. I know you think your life is over, but it is not. Someone helped me get through my troubles and gave me a new life. And He will do the same for you. Can I introduce you to Him?" Curious, he nodded, signaling he wanted to hear more.

My comments provoked the policemen; I had their full attention. One of them knew English and interpreted my statements for the others to understand. Once he comprehended my intentions, he quit interpreting my message and motioned he wanted me to stop speaking. I didn't comply. The other officers asked him why he was waving his hands at me. Mysteriously, he couldn't talk. When he attempted to speak, no words came out. I don't know why that happened. But I know God's ways are often mysterious. I'm convinced God wanted me to preach the Good News to the young man unopposed.

I knew I was taking a significant risk; evangelizing Muslims is illegal in Malaysia. However, the young man was of Indian descent, so he was most likely Hindu. And there was no law against evangelizing Hindus. I must add, though, I shared Jesus and His Gospel with many Muslim policemen while living in Malaysia.

I testified about Jesus and His plan for salvation. Also, how Jesus brought me from a life of destruction to a life overflowing with vitality, purity, joy, peace, and purpose. I encouraged the young man to find a Christian in prison willing to teach him more about Jesus. I could see the young man was moved by my message. He listened intently and nodded with approval. Then, I was taken to an examination room. After being examined, a doctor stated I needed to go to another clinic for an MRI because they didn't have an MRI machine in that facility.

The young man and policemen exited the hospital at the same time we did. With much gratitude, the young man said, "Sir, thank you for your words. I will do as you say and find a Christian in prison." The policemen looked at me with reverence. I believe they were moved by my openness, boldness, and compassion, even though they didn't fully understand my intentions. It was a special moment. God works all things together for those who love and trust Him. This story gets much better.

At the time, I suffered from claustrophobia. Just thinking about being in an MRI machine brought on panic attacks. I asked my doctor to give me a strong sedative before sending me into the MRI machine to ease my anxiety. He graciously complied and assured me the anesthetic would knock me out in seconds.

For me, anesthetics perform like a truth serum. I knew I would passionately share Jesus with my doctor and his assistants before falling asleep. And that's what happened!

When I awoke, my doctor and his assistants, all Muslims, were standing by me with big smiles. They told me I gave a magnificent talk about Jesus and His plan for salvation. My doctor also stated they were moved by our mission work in Malaysia and my plea for Muslims to believe in Jesus. I don't need anesthetics to speak truthfully about God. However, God used that moment to glorify His Son! This story gets better yet!

Later that year, during the Islamic holy month, Ramadan, I received a phone call from my doctor's receptionist. She forwarded an invitation from my doctor to attend his Hari Raya party. Hari Raya is a Muslim festivity at the end of Ramadan. It's as significant to Muslims as Christmas is to Christians.

My doctor was very wealthy and lived in a mansion located in an exclusive neighborhood for the rich and famous. Success did not make him proud are arrogant, though. He remained humble, kind, and gentle, always remembering his roots. Others informed us that he came from an impoverished childhood and never lost sight of his beginnings, which explained his humility.

Upon arrival, we were amazed by the splendor of his property. His mansion and courtyard were lavished with expensive decorations. The cuisine came from the finest restaurants. We noticed all the other guests were arriving in luxury vehicles and limousines. We drove up in a secondhand car.

A servant warmly greeted us, then led us to a table on a patio adorned with exotic flowers and beautiful ornaments. It wasn't long before guests came to greet us. Heads of corporations, high-level government officials, famous celebrities, and even the Prince of Pahang were present. Everyone invited was Muslim, except for us. What an unbelievable honor!

My doctor's wife came and greeted us with joy and respect. She exclaimed, "My husband told me about your mission work in Malaysia. I was deeply moved by your compassion and have shared with the other guests about your work. I admire Oprah's benevolence. You both are like her." We thanked her for her kind words.

Several other guests came to inquire about our mission work in Malaysia. Being Muslim, they were amazed by our boldness and moved by our compassion. They understood very well the dangers of our work. They knew we were Christian missionaries, yet they told us to not lose heart and remain steadfast with our work. Kathy and I sat in their midst and were dumb-founded by what was happening.

As I pondered this event, I realized that fear keeps many Muslims stuck in Islam. There is a genuine hunger for Jesus. The world is waiting to hear the Good News of Salvation. Sadly, fear has closed the mouths of too many missionaries.

God used my reckless driving to reveal His glory at a hospital, a clinic, and a Muslim festivity. God is always intentional and purposeful, despite our shortcomings and missteps! We just need to pay attention.

He said to his disciples, "The harvest is great, but the workers are few. So pray to the Lord who is in charge of the harvest; ask him to send more workers into his fields" (Matthew 9:37-38 - NLT).

Reflections

I have come to believe trials are never an inconvenience. Instead, they are opportunities for indescribable joy (see James 1:2). Amid my trials, I set my gaze on Jesus and trust His loving and faithful guidance.I don't ask my Lord, "Jesus, why did this happen to me?" That only leads to wallowing in self-pity and keeps one stuck in misery.

Instead, I declare who Jesus is over my circumstances, "Lord, you are my Savior and always save me from my troubles. You are my Deliverer and rescue me from my fears.You are my Healer and heal me from my injuries. Lord, I set my gaze upon you alone. Lord, I trust your wisdom and guidance through my trials. Lord, thank you for crowning me with victory by your death and resurrection."Lord, what the devil meant for harm, you will bring goodness" (see Romans 8:28).

I was careless and caused a motorcycle accident. Immediately, I beseeched Jesus for help. I know my God. He is gentle, kind, and merciful. In my heart, I believed Jesus would bring good from my reckless actions. Faith in God's goodness will always reap a harvest of righteousness. And that's what happened. A Hindu found salvation, and the Gospel was preached to police officers, medical staff, and influential Muslims. Only in heaven will I see the fullness of God's goodness that came from my accident.

No matter how difficult your trials and troubles, Jesus is able and willing to turn your anguish into a joyous triumph. Your victory was already paid for on the cross. Hanging on the blessed cross, Jesus cried out, "It is finished" (see John 19:20). Therefore, do not throw away your confidence in Jesus but persevere in battle until you receive the glory of your hope (see Hebrews 10:32-36). And always remember Jesus is forever with you (see Matthew 28:20).

Muslim Parking Lot Attendant Receives Miraculous Healing

We were told it was impossible to get a bank account in Malaysia as a tourist. However, God said ALL things are possible with Him (see Matthew 19:26). Trusting God would grant us a favor, we applied for a bank account, which was accepted. We were delighted to have funds on hand to pay for our bills, daily expenses, and evangelical outreach projects. Until that time, we relied on ATM's which required high fees.

Once deposited in our Malaysian bank account, it took one month to clear our American checks. Consequently, I carefully planned to never come up short with funds. However, on one occasion, our American check still had not cleared six weeks after depositing it. Unfortunately, that caused us to be delinquent on our rent and other bills. Moreover, it was frustrating to hear excuse after excuse from our Malaysian bank why our check had not cleared.

Eventually, our debtors became annoyed with my apologies. Desperate to rectify our predicament, I visited our banker to investigate why our check had not cleared.

As I pulled into the bank's parking lot, an attendant, who happened to be a Muslim, directed me to where I should park. I noticed him limping and wincing in pain as he walked. Also, he wore a brace on his left leg. Parking lot attendants in Malaysia make about 300USD a month, so he probably forced himself to work to support his family despite of his injury.

Overcome with compassion, I asked this man if I could pray in the Name of Jesus for God to heal his leg. It did not matter to him that I was a Christian. He didn't hesitate and complied enthusiastically. He stretched his injured leg forward for prayer without hesitation.

After a short prayer, I asked him to do something with his leg he couldn't do before. Gingerly, he walked in a small circle, applying increasing pressure on his injured leg as he became more confident. Then he started to forcefully stomp on each foot. He was astounded. With a broad smile, he exclaimed that his leg was totally healed.

He then removed his leg brace. I reconfirmed that Jesus healed his leg and, therefore, he should give thanks and praise to Jesus only. He joyfully agreed! Strangely, all my anger over the delinquent deposit vanished. I knew God set up the missing check occurrence so that He could touch that parking lot attendant.

I proceeded into my bank to inquire about the delay. As my banker provided me with another lame explanation, we heard a loud knocking on the bank's window. It was the parking lot attendant. He was ecstatic; his smile stretched from ear to ear. Once he got our attention, He shouted loud enough for us and others in the bank to hear. He thanked and praised Jesus for his healing. He also thanked me for taking the time to pray for him. It was a glorious sight to see this Muslim man praise Jesus, disregarding the risks.

After meeting with my banker, I immediately went outside to exchange contact info with the parking lot attendant. He had already left, and I never saw him again. However, I learned a valuable lesson that day. God works all things together for those who love and trust Him! God misplaced our check so that the Name of Jesus would be lifted high amid all those who witnessed that man's healing. And I must mention, our check cleared shortly later, mysteriously!

"Through faith in the name of Jesus, this man was healed—and you know how crippled he was before. Faith in Jesus' name has healed him before your very eyes (Acts 3:16—NLT).

Reflections

Our response to an offense will always determine our fate. When we are wronged by someone, God requires that we sincerely forgive them. And when we do, God will heal and restore our souls. Holding a grudge will always keep us stuck in misery. Complaining, grumbling, criticizing, or judging is symptoms of bitterness. These symptoms bring darkness to our souls. They also give access to evil spirits whose purpose is to bring torment and destruction.

Moreover, a bitter spirit is a significant hindrance to receiving victory. Abiding in resurrection power found on the Cross of Calvary is needed to heal, restore, and redeem what was broken. This power was made possible by God's forgiveness of our sins and is only available when we abide in a spirit of forgiveness.

Though my Malaysian banks' action was a minor offense, I responded inappropriately by grumbling, complaining, and criticizing. Gratefully, God is merciful and allowed me to come to my senses. Compassion consumed me when I saw the Muslim parking lot attendant tormented with pain. His infliction made my troubles seem petty. I repented of my anger and sought God for forgiveness and cleansing. Consequently, not only did Jesus miraculously heal the parking lot attendant, but He also removed my offense and gave me favor with my bank.

Early in my walk with Jesus, He taught me how to receive total inner healing from wrongdoings, no matter how horrendous. Jesus said, "Mark, when you possess my compassion for your enemies, then you will no longer bear the pain of their offense."

Early in my spiritual walk with Jesus, I was falsely accused and sent to jail. That turned out to be an enormous blessing. Sitting in jail was the place that Jesus taught me to love my enemies, do good things for those who hate me, bless those who curse me, and pray for those who hurt me (see Luke 6:27-28).

Daily, I take time to remember how Jesus paid a horrendous price to forgive all the sins I committed against God and others. Doing so always brings me to a place of immense gratitude. Moreover, it inspires me to forgive others, no matter the severity of their offense. This lesson has been invaluable on the mission field. We are constantly slandered, backstabbed, mocked, and persecuted.

If you are looking for justice in a situation and have not found it, perhaps you are holding onto an offense. Any hint of bitterness will be a hindrance to receiving justice. If you allow Jesus to bring you to a place of compassion for those who hate or oppose you, God will give healing, restoration, and redemption. Following is a prayer I have prayed many times. I hope it brings comfort to others.

Dear Lord Jesus,

Thank you for taking my place on the cross and receiving eternal judgment for my sins. Your love and mercy are indescribable! Lord, I confess I have not shown this same mercy to others or myself. Instead, I have harbored bitterness, grudges, and resentment in my soul. Lord, I choose to forgive every person who has offended and hurt me. Lord, I release them to your loving care, and I release my right to hold onto offenses. Lord, flood my heart with compassion for my enemies. Whenever I'm tempted to revisit offenses, Lord, remind me to pray a blessing over those who have hurt me. Thank you for cleansing my heart from the poison of bitterness. Thank you for flooding my heart with compassion for those I have held with contempt. Lord, your grace and mercy are amazing! Amen & Halleluiah!

Muslim Professor Puts His Faith in Jesus to Save His Son

Restaurants have always been one of our favorite places to evangelize. We have many beautiful testimonies of God touching people with His love in restaurants, both in America and other countries. One such time, while on an evangelical outreach in Eastern Malaysia, we were compelled to stop at a quaint roadside café for a meal. In hindsight, the Holy Spirit most definitely guided us to that location. Our visit that day initiated a bizarre sequence of events.

Soon after sitting, we met the establishment owner (Badia), a pleasant Muslim woman with a gentle spirit. Kathy is bold, passionate, and gentle in her witness for others to know Jesus. Kathy also knows how to use the gift of prophecy to bring the lost to Jesus. Kathy shared with Badia what God was showing her about Badia's troubled life.

Stunned by the accuracy of Kathy's 'word of knowledge.' Badia shouted to all in her restaurant, "This lady is a prophetess.I must sit with her and hear what she has to say—forgive me, but I cannot serve anyone now." Badia then sat down with Kathy to hear more. As Kathy continued to share what God had placed on her heart, Badia sat mesmerized, hanging on Kathy's every word.

After sharing her heart, Kathy asked Badia if she could pray a blessing over her in the Name of Jesus. Badia enthusiastically accepted Kathy's invitation. Though these are awkward moments, it did not matter to Badia that she allowed a Christian woman to pray for her; God had opened her heart to receive His love. The customers did not understand what was happening. However, they showed reverence for what God was doing. God's glory had pierced through the kingdom of darkness, opening the door for us to evangelize.

We told Badia we would return to her restaurant on our next visit to Eastern Malaysia. We could see in her eyes a deep hunger to know us. She had an encounter with God's glory and desperately craved more.

The following month our son, Justin, came from America to visit us and experience Malaysia. Justin joined us on several evangelical outreaches in Malaysia and Indonesia, including our return trip to Badia's restaurant in Eastern Malaysia.

Our spiritual sons, who translated for us, needed a break, so we embarked on our journey, trusting God would provide translators when necessary. We still could not speak the language well enough for in-depth conversations.

On the way to the restaurant in Eastern Malaysia, we stopped at several houses to visit those we had shared Jesus with on prior evangelical outreaches. We always brought with us Bibles for those who wanted one. Smuggling Bibles is illegal in Malaysia and carries severe penalties for those found guilty. With Justin, we went through seven different police checkpoints. Miraculously, the police would pass us through each time without searching our car. That was an extraordinary miracle for two reasons. First, the police put out a warrant for our arrest circulating in that region. Second, the police searched everyone's vehicle at each checkpoint except ours. When we arrived at the restaurant, Badia introduced us to her husband, Mohamed. Mohamed was an English Instructor at a local college; thus, God provided us the perfect translator. Suspicious of our intentions, Mohamed asked if he could sit and talk with us. I did not want to endanger Justin, so I kept our chat superficial and refrained from evangelism. I felt sowing seeds of kindness was appropriate for the circumstances. However, God had other plans!

After a delightful discussion about world events, I rose and politely told Mohamed we had to depart for our home, a seven-hour drive. Mohamed would not let me go; he put his hand on my shoulder and gently pushed me into my chair. Then Mohamed looked deep into my eyes and, with a solemn voice, said, "You and your wife were here before. Your wife had words for my wife." I was startled by his distraught demeanor; I thought we were in trouble. However, I had peace. God was with us. Moreover, these encounters were excellent opportunities to reveal Jesus and His plan for salvation.

With a mixture of compassion and unease, I leaned forward and replied, "Yes, we were here last month, and my wife had words from our God for your wife." I expected a sharp rebuke from Mohamed; he looked irate. But that wasn't the case; he had a broken heart and sought comfort.

With sad eyes and a quivering voice, Mohamed asked me, "Does your wife have any words from your God about me?" My heart ached for him; Mohamed's grief and hopelessness were evident, and he sought encouragement. And it did not matter to him that we were Christians. Gently, I replied, "She might have words for you, but I have a word for you from my God." With a curious look, Mohamed waited for me to continue.

I shared with Mohamed what I thought I heard from God. I said, "Your eldest son has run away. He's a drug user, he steals to get money, and he hangs out with a bad crowd." I paused to see if Mohamed would acknowledge my words were actual or not. I could not read him; he remained silent and motionless, glaring into my eyes. My heart raced, and my fearful thoughts wanted to betray the moment, "If my words are not from God, we are all in big trouble."

Nevertheless, I decided to swing for a grand slam and shared more with Mohamed what God shared with me. I said, "Mohamed, many times you went to the mosque and prayed to Allah to save your son, only to be disappointed again and again. You have come to a place of despair and hopelessness; you are miserable.

Mohamed, I love you too much not to tell you the truth. I see you are an educated man and know about the Christian Triune God. I am here to tell you it is true; Jesus is God's eternal son. And only Jesus can save your son. Mohamed, the next time you go to your mosque, I encourage you not to pray to Allah, but to pray to my God, and pray this way—'Jesus, if you are the Son of God, please save my son from destruction and bring him home.' If you pray this way, my God will do a miracle and bring your son to his senses and save him from destruction. But, when your son does return, don't scold, or lecture him, only love him."

I then shared the story about the prodigal son in the Bible with Mohamed. And I told Mohamed about God's magnificent plan for salvation through His eternal Son, Jesus. By God's grace I continued to express my faith through love (see Galatians 5:6). Genuine love is always a powerful weapon to demolish deceptive strongholds.

After pouring out my heart, I hoped Mohamed would acknowledge that my words were spot on. He did not. He sat motionlessly and glared at me with the same painful expression. Sensing it was time to depart, we said our goodbyes. Mohamed and his wife graciously thanked us for our visit; that was encouraging.

We returned to visit Mohamed and Badia at their restaurant the following month only to find it closed. So, we decided to visit one of our new disciples, Ahmed, who lived in the same city. We led Ahmed, a government immigration officer, to Jesus several months earlier.

When we arrived at Ahmed's house, we were startled by his greeting. Smiling, Ahmed inquired, "Did you stop at Mohamed and Badia's restaurant? I thought to myself, "How did Ahmed know we had a relationship with them?" Ahmed continued to ask questions, "Did you notice their café is closed for the weekend? Do you want to know why?"

It is perilous for a Muslim to acknowledge they converted to Christianity. Still shocked, I replied, "I'm surprised to hear you are friends with Mohamed. Yes, what's going on with him and his family? Why is their restaurant closed?"

Mohamed had shared all the details about our visits to Badia's cafe with Ahmed. Furthermore, Mohamed told Ahmed all my prophecy about his son was true. Convicted by my words, Mohamed followed my advice, went to the mosque, and prayed, "Jesus, if you are the Son of God, save my son and bring him home." Shortly later, miraculously, Mohamed's son came to his senses and returned home with a broken and contrite heart. Encouraged by his son's remarkable transformation, Mohamed called a friend, a senior official at a police academy, to enroll his son. Mohamed, Badia, and their son traveled to the city where the police academy was located. That was the reason for their restaurant not being closed.

We sat down in a roadside restaurant for a meal. Prompted by the Holy Spirit, Kathy shared a word with the Muslim owner with boldness and compassion. Kathy's words became God's seed to plant the realities of His kingdom in many hearts and reveal the majesty of Jesus! God's plans are always more powerful than anything we can imagine. Following the guidance of the Holy Spirit will always bring heaven to earth, as it is in heaven.

A spiritual gift is given to each of us so we can help each other. To one person the Spirit gives the ability to give wise advice; to another the same Spirit gives a message of special knowledge. The same Spirit gives great faith to another, and to someone else the one Spirit gives the gift of healing. He gives one person the power to perform miracles, and another the ability to prophesy. He gives someone else the ability to discern whether a message is from the Spirit of God or from another spirit. Still another person is given the ability to speak in unknown languages, while another is given the ability to interpret what is being said. It is the one and only Spirit who distributes all these gifts. He alone decides which gift each person should have
(1 Corinthians 8:7-11 - NLT).

Reflections

I have heard many times, "God will never give you anything you cannot handle." In essence, that is not true. God often gives us tasks that seemingly appear impossible by our own abilities. Only when we humble ourselves before our Lord will He exalt us to accomplish His will.

Moses, Gideon, and many other biblical figures believed they were the wrong person to fulfill God's instructions successfully. God chose them because of their humility and willingness to trust and obey God wholly.

Faith in Jesus alone is all we need to fulfill God's plans and purposes. Any measure of confidence in our education, character, spiritual maturity, past experiences, skin color, or anything else is misplaced faith and will hinder fulfilling God's will.

When God told us to visit Badia a second time, I thought to myself, "How's this going to work? Our spiritual sons who interpret for us are taking a break, and our understanding of the Malay language is limited." Knowing my thoughts, God replied, "Mark, I will provide everything you need for success." Instantly, I smiled and believed God would provide an Interpreter.

Upon arriving at Badia's restaurant, her husband, Mohamed, greeted us with perfect English; no Interpreter was needed. As I shared from my heart, Mohamed believed my message about Jesus. Consequently, God restored Mohamed and Badia's relationship with their beloved son. Even more extraordinary, they tasted Jesus' goodness. I genuinely believe they became "Believers."

Perhaps God has called you to accomplish a specific purpose. But you are hesitant to proceed because you feel unqualified, unprepared, too weak, not worthy, or the timing is wrong.

Don't lose heart. Humble yourself before our Lord, and He will exalt you at the right time (see James 4:10).

Never put your faith in your natural abilities—that is prideful. God opposes the proud but gives grace to the humble (see James 4:6). And only by God's grace are we able to fulfill His plans and purposes.

God chooses the foolish, by human standards, to shame those who believe they are wise. And he selects those who know they are weak to shame those who think they are strong (see 1 Corinthians 1:27).

Banana Tree Leads a Muslim Immigration Officer to Jesus

While in Malaysia, we trained many Malaysians to share the Good News, primarily by example on the mission field. Two spiritual sons, former Muslims, had been with us on many evangelical outreaches and learned well. We taught them to always help the poor, pray for the sick, and share the gospel on every occasion. We sensed they were ready to embark on a mission trip without us. So, we laid hands on them and prayed God would anoint them for success. Then as proud parents, we sent them.

They were excited to share all that happened during their evangelical outreach upon their return. Not leaving out a single detail, our sons exuberantly shared how God empowered them to boldly preach the gospel and to show the poor extravagant generosity. It's always more gratifying to see our children flourish than ourselves. We rejoiced with them.

They wanted us to see the fruit of their efforts. So, our spiritual sons asked us to join them to meet an immigration officer, Ahmed. They claimed Ahmed had an open heart for Jesus and believed he was ready to follow Jesus Christ as his Lord and Savior. I mentioned Ahmed in my previous story.

It was a seven-hour drive to Ahmed's house; he lived in a beautiful city nestled next to the South China Sea. Upon arrival, Ahmed warmly greeted our sons and us. However, I noticed his wife was displeased by our visit. Fearful of persecution, she did not want to be associated with Christian missionaries evangelizing in her city. Nevertheless, her sour disposition didn't stop her husband from requesting we stay for fellowship, refreshments, and snacks.

As we sat at their kitchen table, the Holy Spirit reminded Kathy of a dream she had the night before. Sensing her dream had something to do with Ahmed and his wife, she shared it.

In her dream, Kathy saw a severe storm with powerful winds. Then, she saw a mighty gust blow down a large banana tree, destroying a house. Kathy carries a royalty about herself, so nobody brushes her off when she speaks. Ahmed pondered her words, wondering what they might mean, so did we.

We stayed at a nearby motel that evening. While we were sleeping, a severe storm with mighty winds woke us up. Naturally, we all remembered Kathy's dream and pondered what it meant.

The following morning, we returned to Ahmed's home. We were stunned to see that a large banana tree had fallen and destroyed a significant part of his house. Ahmed was hysterical and disoriented. The fulfillment of Kathy's dream shook Ahmed to the core of his being.

Convicted by this tragic event, Ahmed had a lot of questions about Jesus and His plan for salvation. We emphasized that our God didn't cause that natural disaster, but He will bring goodness from destruction for those who love and trust Him. We told Ahmed we would raise funds to help him repair all the damage. Kathy's prophetic dream, benevolence, and the Good News of Salvation profoundly impacted Ahmed.

After a few more visits, Ahmed decided to become a follower of Jesus. As he surrendered his life to Jesus, he wept. We did too. Then he looked at me and, with a broad smile, said, "Mark, we are now brothers in Jesus." We rejoiced and gave each other big hugs.

However, I could see his wife was infuriated by her husband's conversion. It appeared she was already planning his and our demise.

Before we left, we gave Ahmed a Bible and told him we would teach him God's Word. Though it is illegal to provide Bibles for Muslims in Malaysia, we smuggled Bibles everywhere we traveled. Ahmed was overcome with emotion when he held his new Bible.

The next several months met with Ahmed often. He really enjoyed his new faith in Jesus and loved reading his Bible. Ahmed is a brilliant man with an affable personality. However, persecution was standing at his door. Which always comes for Muslims who convert to Christianity.

I called Ahmed to inform him we would visit him in a couple of days. Ahmed responded hysterically; he shouted, "Do not come to my place anymore. I have been reported to the Islamic Religious Police, and so have you. They are constantly watching my place. And they will arrest you and your wife if they see you in my city." I asked Ahmed who reported him and us to the religious police. He didn't know. Though I have no evidence, I believe his wife did to save herself.

Fearful the authorities had tapped his phone, he wanted to hang up. Ahmed bitterly wept. My heart ached for him. Before we ended our conversation, I asked Ahmed if he still had his Bible. Still grieving, Ahmed replied, "My Bible is my treasure. The authorities will never find it." Ahmed took a significant risk just to talk with me on the phone.

We never heard from Ahmed again. However, we led a clan of seven families to salvation who lived only a short distance from his house. Over the years, when we would visit those families who lived close by, I would take time to discreetly drive-by Ahmed's house, praying a blessing over him and his family. My heart ached to see him. And I know he felt the same way.

Kathy and I trust Jesus will never leave nor forsake Ahmed. His surrender was as genuine as any I have observed.

In the last days,' God says, 'I will pour out my Spirit upon all people. Your sons and daughters will prophesy. Your young men will see visions, and your old men will dream dreams. In those days I will pour out my Spirit even on my servants—men and women alike—and they will prophesy,' (see Acts 2:17-18 - NLT).

Reflections

God poured out His Spirit on everyone so that we would see visions, have dreams, and prophesy. These divine abilities have been vital for our ministry. At times, God used dreams and visions to bring a warning, correction, guidance, and/or understanding. When Kathy and I committed to growing in this dimension, we saw God's plans and purposes more clearly.

Kathy's dream about the banana tree was instrumental in bringing salvation to Ahmed. In his anguish, Ahmed sought understanding. Kathy explained that our God gives visions and dreams because He loves and cares for us. God allowed the banana tree to fall on Ahmed's house to reveal His glory and bring Ahmed salvation. We were able to raise money to repair Ahmed's house. That act of benevolence demonstrated God's love, and ours was sincere.

I want to emphasize the importance of seeking and growing in the prophetic gift for all Believers. It has been a priceless blessing in our personal life and ministry. Moreover, God instructs us to earnestly seek the gift of prophecy (see 1 Corinthians 14:1).

Iranian College Student
Discovers "Living Water"

We had just experienced a bitter disappointment. We were crushed! We felt betrayed by several spiritual sons who we deeply loved and trusted. We were reclaiming ground for Jesus with them in dark, dangerous regions. We knew Satan would attack us for bringing God's kingdom into his strongholds. We were accustomed to constant spiritual warfare, but this betrayal deeply hurt.

Demonic forces are constantly working to divide and destroy relationships. Pride led our sons to abandon us. Though, I'm sure my shortcomings exacerbated the conflict.

Feeling overwhelmed with disappointment, I needed time alone with God to pray and sort things out.

I told Kathy I wanted to go to a forested park and spend time with Jesus and her only. She agreed, so we visited a large park known to have miles and miles of walking trails through jungle terrain. I was resolute not to minister to anyone we met. I was too demoralized and needed time to renew and strengthen my spirit in God's presence. However, Jesus had other plans!

As we walked on a trail, a young Iranian man (Farhad) hastily approached us; he was hysterical. Frantically, he lamented, "I am dying of thirst, and I do not know where to get a drink of water. I am begging you, could you please help me?" Thankfully, he spoke English.

Many Iranians attend college in Malaysia for affordable education. Farhad was pursuing a master's degree in science in a city about a four-hour drive away. He had come to Kuala Lumpur earlier that morning to meet his wife (Darya) at the airport later that night. They were newly married and had not seen each other in six months. He decided to take a walk in the park to fill in the time until her arrival.

Compassion for this young man replaced all my moaning. I told Farhad, "I noticed a vendor on the path a short walk from where we stand. I will buy a cold bottle of water for you to drink. I also want to tell you about 'living water.' And if you were to drink of this 'living water,' you would never thirst again." Farhad was overcome with gratitude and intrigued to hear about this 'living water.'

As we sat and quenched our thirst, I shared the story about the Samaritan woman at the well with Jesus. He was captivated by my story and hung onto my every word. Also, I shared the meaning of 'living water.' As I did, I intertwined my testimony, who Jesus is, and the purpose of His crucifixion. Bible stories and personal testimonies are powerful evangelical tools.

Overcome, Farhad begged us to meet him and his wife later that evening at a restaurant. He wanted his wife to hear about Jesus too. We enthusiastically agreed and exchanged phone numbers.

Later that evening, Kathy and I met with Farhad and Darya. They were Muslims but had open minds. She was not wearing a Muslim head covering, which Islamic law requires. She stated that she wanted to express some freedom while away from Iran. However, the Islamic authorities in Malaysia require the same for Muslim women. Darya is a free-spirited soul, so she was willing to take the risk.

I always ask the Holy Spirit to guide my thoughts and words before I testify about Jesus because everyone has different personalities and backgrounds. An approach that may have been successful with someone in the past might not be the right approach presently. Holy Spirit's guidance is vital in all aspects of ministry, so I am always seeking His promptings.

Holy Spirit compelled me to share with Farhad and Darya from Ephesians 5:21-33. This scripture instructs husbands and wives how to love and honor one another. Its message is contrary to what Muslims believe about marriage. The Islamic faith states that men are superior to women; hence, wives should be treated as inferior partners. From Ephesians, I shared that a husband is a leader in the marriage. But their actions will be righteous in God's eyes only when they put their wife's best interest and needs above their own. In essence, God will be pleased only when husbands show their wives sacrificial love, gentleness, kindness, and patience. Neither Farhad nor Darya was offended by my words.

Inspired by my teaching, Darya playfully hit Farhad and, with a broad smile, said, "Listen to this man and obey this teaching from Jesus." We all laughed, but Kathy and I sensed she sincerely wanted her husband to adopt that teaching. God's Word opened their hearts to hear and learn more about Jesus and His kingdom.

Though they believed our testimony of Jesus was real, fear kept them from being Christ's followers. And their concerns are legit. Three other Iranians we led to Jesus cannot return to Iran because Iranian authorities would kill them for converting to Christianity. They chose Jesus over their families, friends, communities, and country. It takes time for God to perfect His love in their hearts, which casts out all fear (see 1 John 4:18). We need to be patient and allow God's love to flow through us, perfecting His love in their hearts.

As mentioned, Farhad and Darya lived in a city that was a four-hour drive from ours. We visited them when time allowed. However, our ministry had quickly multiplied in other areas of Malaysia. We needed to focus our time, energy, and resources on discipling those we led to Jesus. Hence, our connection with Farhad and Darya faded over time. Nevertheless, we placed numerous kingdom seeds in their hearts and trusted God would bring others to water those seeds.

After sharing the Gospel of Salvation, we have seen many Muslims believe our testimony to be true. However, fear of rejection and persecution from their families and communities prevented them from being Christ's disciples.

Nevertheless, some Muslims we shared the Gospel with decided later to be Christ's followers. They shared that our sacrificial, crazy love compelled them to leave Islam and become faithful disciples of Jesus. Love never quits, endures through all trials, and always finds a way to victory.

Muslim evangelism and discipleship make for a perilous and challenging ministry. We endure ongoing threats, trials, and troubles. Only by God's Spirit do we have success. Moreover, our rewards make our suffering worthy. We love what we do!

Wonderfully, God restored our relationship with our spiritual sons who abandoned us. Until this day, we are in a close relationship with them.

I learned a valuable lesson; even when I feel defeated and empty, God can use me!

Jesus replied, "If you only knew the gift God has for you and whom you are speaking to, you would ask me, and I would give you living water," (John 4:19 - NLT).

Reflections

We should never allow our emotions to influence our faith, only God's Word. Often, my feelings have betrayed me. Fear, doubt, and bitterness are demonic powers that will bring darkness to our souls if we give them a place of influence. Their motive is to pervert God's will and bring destruction.

When I felt betrayed by our spiritual sons, I grieved deeply and struggled with resentment. Feeling defeated, I told God I would not witness that day. However, God was not deterred by my weakness. Instead, God used my shortcomings as an opportunity to meet a thirsty Iranian college student.

Seeing how desperate the Iranian student was, compassion swiftly replaced self-pity. And beautifully, God's grace brought me to my senses. Consequently, not only did the Iranian and his wife receive a blessing, but so did I; God healed my broken heart.

If I had allowed my feelings to lead me, I would have lost an opportunity to glorify God. I am grateful for God's patience and gentleness. He overcomes me!

Horrifically Demonized
Nine-Year-Old Girl is Set Free

We were driving from Sabah to Sarawak in Borneo, one of the largest islands in the world. As we traversed mountainous roads through jungle terrain, our car relentlessly bounced and swayed, straining to stay on the road. On the nine-hour journey, we prayed, worshipped, told stories, and at times, quietly pondered all God was going to do. Not knowing at the time, this mission trip was the seed that led to a massive revival, bringing multiple indigenous tribes together a year later.

One of our spiritual sons, Jaffar (former Muslim), had arranged this mission trip to Sarawak. Jaffar pastored a church in Sandakan, Sabah. One of his church leaders, a young mother from the Lun Bawang tribe, invited us to Sarawak to minister to her family and community.

Lun Bawang means 'people of the country' or 'native people.' We always felt honored when invited to bring the gospel to those who live in spiritually dark and remote regions and are too poor to pay a guest evangelist. We were thrilled to serve the beautiful Lun Bawang tribe, especially after hearing how eager they were for us to come.

Once we arrived in Sarawak, from early morning to late in the evening, we went from village to village, and house to house, ministering to multitudes of hungry souls. The Lun Bawang people received us with arms wide open; they were desperate to receive a divine touch from Jesus. And God did not deny them a blessing. He could not resist their humility and hunger and generously poured out His blessings at every meeting.

Before our first engagement one early morning, Jaffar told us a shocking story that broke our hearts. Jaffar expressed, "A severely demonized nine-year-old Lun Bawang girl is causing massive fear in this region. She lives with her family close to where we will be today. Christians tried to cast out the evil spirits but were unsuccessful; the small girl overcame them by the evil power dwelling in her. Her family lives in terror and suffering. She bites and hits her family members and screams for hours.

Furthermore, an evil spirit prophesizes through her. The demon communicates with other demons who follow her family members when they leave their house. When they return home, she gives a detailed account of their every movement, causing much fear in the family. Sadly, testimonies of her possession have caused terror to spread throughout the entire region, and no one outside of her family dares to come to their house, including a local pastor."

The horrific plight of this family struck us to the core. I was outraged by the torment Satan had brought. I sensed God wanted us to cast out those demons and minister to her family.So, I instructed Jaffar to cancel all our upcoming appointments and immediately take us to the demonized girl's house. I stated that we would not leave until she was set free.

Jesus commands His disciples to cast out demons in His Name; therefore, this is part of our mission work.I could not live with myself if we proceeded with our schedule at the expense of this family not receiving redemption. Especially when we knew we had the faith, authority, and power to help!

Jaffar complied immediately, and we proceeded to the demonized girl's house. We pulled up to a dilapidated shack in the jungle. Akat and Rikan, the parents of the possessed girl (Aida), warmly greeted us. Their countenance spoke loudly of their pain, despair, and hopelessness. They were sullen and downcast; it was an awkward moment. Nevertheless, with sensitivity, we stated the purpose of our visit.

God gave us unusual faith to accomplish this assignment. Compassionately, I told Akat and Rikan we would stay and minister to their daughter until the evil spirits were cast out. Not wanting to be offensive, they politely accepted our ministry. However, it was apparent my words brought them little comfort or hope. They stated that other Christians had already tried to set their daughter free but were harshly defeated. Akat and Rikan were crushed and exhausted!

It was vital to find and close the door that allowed the evil spirits to enter, so we asked the parents many probing questions. In the United States and other countries, we have ministered to many children who needlessly suffered because their parents unintentionally opened demonic doors (see Hosea 4:6). However, harsh correction is never good ministry. Only when faith flows through compassion will we have success, for that is the heart of God (see Galatians 5:6)!

As missionaries, one of our responsibilities is to teach God's ways—even if those we minister to don't follow Christianity! It's incredible how many people of other cultures and faiths are convicted by biblical teachings!

Akat shared a story that revealed his error and led to their suffering. He and his family had traveled to another city where his brother lived. His brother, a high-level witch doctor, gave him a ceremonial sword as a gift. Akat's brother used that sword in rituals to invoke spirits. Akat accepted the sword and put it in their car to bring home as a cherished gift.

While they were traveling home, Aida suddenly became violent. In an instant, she transformed from a mild-mannered, bubbly girl to belligerent and violent. They tried to calm her down, but all their efforts failed. Never had their daughter exhibited this terrifying behavior. They were horrified!

Akat and Rikan had a simple understanding of Jesus and His gospel. However, they did not know the Bible states that an object used in ceremonial rituals to invoke spirits could become a door for demons to enter. I shared the following scriptures with them:

"You must burn their idols in fire, and you must not covet the silver or gold that covers them. You must not take it, or it will become a trap to you, for it is detestable to the Lord your God. Do not bring any detestable objects into your home, for then you will be destroyed, just like them. You must utterly detest such things, for they are set apart for destruction." (Deuteronomy 7:25-26 NLT).

"…And do not let your people practice fortune-telling, or use sorcery, or interpret omens, or engage in witchcraft, or cast spells, or function as mediums or psychics, or call forth the spirits of the dead" (Deuteronomy 18:10-11 NLT).

I explained to the parents that whenever we seek supernatural power, wisdom, guidance, or favor from any source other than the Holy Spirit, we open the door for evil spirits. And their purpose is to steal, kill, and destroy (see John 10:10). God's Word convicted their hearts; they repented and prayed for forgiveness. And as I mentioned, shame has no place or purpose when we enter the throne of grace.

Tenderly, I assured Akat and Rikan, "When we confess our sins, Heavenly Father is eager to cleanse us of all unrighteousness (see John 1:9). Moreover, Jesus became a curse for us, empowering us to live under God's blessings! Wonderfully, all God's children possess the authority to break all curses, in the Name of Jesus (see Galatians 3:23)." Akat and Rikan were eager to learn and comply.

The first night we attempted to cast out the demons didn't go well; we failed. Aida viciously manifested demonic behavior. Sadly, the small measure of hope the parents had left. However, love never quits, never surrenders, but always perseveres until it reigns victoriously. And that divine love consumes us. Moreover, Jesus paid the price for all our victories on the Cross at Calvary. We only need to persevere in battle until victory is secured.

We were determined to press into the heavenly realm until God reached down with His mighty right hand and cast out the demons. We decided to rest for the night and proceed with deliverance the following day. We would not leave until that precious child was set free.

That night, as we were resting at a nearby home, I beseeched God for wisdom and guidance for what to do the following morning. God faithfully responded and gave me specific instructions.

The following morning, we followed the Lord's advice. At first, the demons tried to manifest, causing Aida to scream and growl. In Jesus Name, I commanded them to be silent. The demons caused Aida to immediately go into a deep slumber. After six hours of ministry, suddenly, Aida awoke from her comatose state. Her cheerful countenance had returned—all the demons were cast out.

It was a magnificent sight; God's glory had pierced the darkness and brought deliverance to this beloved child. Aida's family went crazy with joy, seeing that their precious daughter was back to her spunky, playful self. Their exuberant celebration was a sight to behold we will never forget.

Like a mighty wind, God's Spirit swept away chaos and despair and flooded the atmosphere with indescribable peace and joy. Overcome by God's goodness, we all sang songs of praise and thanksgiving. Akat and Rikan got their beloved daughter back. Aida's older brother and younger sister were present—they got their sister back. I've never seen a happier family, ever! They were beyond ecstatic; no words can appropriately describe the joy. For the remainder of the day, we continued to rejoice with them.

Akat and Rikan gave us beautiful hand-crafted gifts from their culture to signify everlasting friendship. Oh, it was an extraordinary celebration!

I don't know why it took so long to cast out the demons. Most likely, to defeat that kind of demonic presence required greater faith than we had. We needed to endure in prayer and fasting until we had enough faith to succeed (see Matthew 17:19-20).

We blessed their house for ministry, and until this day, their home is a "House of Prayer" and a blessing to multitudes. This deliverance took place in 2016, and Aida is still free to this day!

The testimony of Aida's deliverance spread like wildfire in that region. Everyone knew of her possession and praised God for her salvation. Inspired by her deliverance, Christian leaders from the Lun Bawang tribe and several other indigenous tribes invited us to conduct a three-day revival/healing meeting the following year. They were eager to have a fresh encounter with God. We gladly accepted their invitation.

It was a powerful three days and nights of ministry. God poured out His glory on all our meetings; multitudes found salvation, deliverance, and divine healings. So many wondrous things happened those three days that will be another story!

During that three-day conference, the Holy Spirit compelled me to teach many local pastors and leaders about the dangers of syncretism. Syncretism is the merging of different religious beliefs and practices that oppose one another. Their flocks professed Jesus as their Lord and Savior. At the same time, they continued to practice their pagan rituals of animism, witchcraft, and sorcery. Syncretism is a common practice I have seen around the world, including in the United States. It's also a significant reason why God sent us to other nations - to bring correction, repentance, deliverance, and healing caused by such evil practices.

As we visited the Lun Bawang tribe, our schedule had been set with many house visits. God had other plans; His are always better.

You cannot drink the cup of the Lord and the cup of demons. You cannot partake of the table of the Lord and the table of demons. Shall we provoke the Lord to jealousy? Are we stronger than he, (1 Corinthians 10:21-22 - NLT)?

Reflections

Ignorance of God's Word is dangerous. The road of deception has many traps waiting to ensnare those who choose to fulfill their carnal desires. Consequently, those who remain ignorant and defiant will needlessly suffer from demonic oppression and torment. In contrast, God's Word is a light unto the path for those who hunger for truth. And those who walk in divine light will enjoy immeasurable blessings.

Our Heavenly Father is supernatural and desires that ALL His children possess supernatural abilities. Therefore, it is perfectly natural to seek miraculous signs and wonders. However, God's Word warns that we should only seek supernatural power, guidance, favor, or other manifestations from the Holy Spirit.

From Deuteronomy 15:10-13, God's Word explicitly forbids engagement in the following: divination, sorcery, interpreting omens, witchcraft, casting spells, mediums, spiritual readings, or consulting dead spirits. God calls these practices detestable. Why? Because they do not open the door for Holy Spirit, but rather, for demonic spirits. God calls these practices spiritual adultery (see Hosea 4:10).

Our culture is filled with games, movies, media, and entertainment steeped in forbidden practices. Sadly, many churches have compromised their faith by not teaching these matters. Rarely have I heard a sermon from a pastor teaching on the occult. Christian leaders must heed God's warning:

My people are destroyed for lack of knowledge; because you have rejected knowledge, I reject you from being a priest to me. And since you have forgotten the law of your God, I also will forget your children (Hosea 4:6 - ESV).

When I was a teenager, I engaged in several forbidden activities. I was curious to experience supernatural power. There was nothing wrong with that; however, my ignorance led to disobedience and much suffering. I am grateful Heavenly Father brought me understanding and deliverance. I confessed my sins, and He mercifully cleansed me of all unrighteousness by the precious Blood of His Son, Jesus (see 1 John1:9).

In 2000, God called us to open our home for ministry. Multitudes came and found healing and freedom from the bondage of sin. However, before we opened our house, God showed us all the detestable things He wanted us to throw out. Consequently, God's glory found a place in our home to dwell, which was required for effective and powerful ministry.

I cannot overemphasize the importance of hearing and obeying God's Word on these matters. If you have not gone through spiritual cleansing for yourself and your house, I encourage you to do so. Evil spirits exist, and their purpose is to steal, kill, and destroy (see John 10:10). God's Word clearly states that forbidden objects can be the doorway for demons to bring destruction to your house (see Deuteronomy 7:25-26). Moreover, evil has a legal right to dwell where there is darkness. True confession and repentance must always be accompanied by righteous living.

Wealthy Muslim Gives Us
His Luxury Apartment

Unexpected trouble comes to everyone, at times with no good outcome in sight. Amid our trials, we have two opposing choices that will determine our fate—fear or faith. Fear always leads to despair, hopelessness, and misery. However, persevering faith always leads to a glorious outcome. Amid our trials, we should not lean on our own understanding. Instead, we should trust God and seek His wisdom and guidance (see Proverbs 3:5-6). Moreover, we should always keep in mind the outcome of our trials might not be what we envisioned. Nevertheless, God's ways are always superior.

Our trials can be magnificent opportunities for inexpressible joy (see James 1:2-3). When life squeezes us, either godly or ungodly character will come forth. When trials expose our weaknesses and character flaws, they become fantastic opportunities for spiritual growth. If we set our focus firmly on Jesus and His mercy, with thanksgiving and praise, God will bless us with divine wisdom and grace.Moreover, God will use these trials to strengthen and perfect our faith.

Amid trials, Satan will always tempt us to take our eyes off Jesus and focus on a negative outcome; we must not come under his dominion of influence. Satan wants to feed us anxiety, discouragement, and despair. That's what happened to the Israelites in the desert; Satan destroyed their faith. Consequently, they did not receive God's promises and died in the wilderness.

When we set our gaze upon Jesus amid our battles, our faith and hope will soar to new heights, and the impossible will become possible. Amid our struggles, we should never throw away our confidence in Jesus which is more precious than gold.

This story is about a trial we had in Malaysia. On the grand scale of things, it wasn't much of a problem. However, it beautifully demonstrates God's faithfulness for those who trust Him to make an impossible situation possible.

While ministering in Australia, I received a phone call from our Malaysian landlord. He is an economizer of words and got straight to the point, "Mark, I have sold my rental house, and you have two weeks to move out." Malaysian laws are often different from American laws. We had no recourse except to comply. In appearance, our predicament looked hopeless. We still had one week of ministry in Australia. By the time we arrived home, we would only have one week to find and secure another residence, pack our whole household, and move. We needed a miracle.

Immediately after the phone call, I wrestled with an offense. "How could our landlord be so rude," I thought! However, the Holy Spirit encouraged us to pray for and bless our landlord, so we did.

As we worshipped Jesus, He brought us to a beautiful place of faith and peace. Worship is one way we humble ourselves before God. And when we draw close to God, He draws close to us, and the devil flees (see James 4:7-9). By faith, we thanked Jesus for our new residence.

Following our time of praise and prayer, the Holy Spirit prompted me to send a message to all our friends in Malaysia, informing them of our dilemma. God is so good and faithful when we set our hope on Jesus!

A few days later, while still ministering in Australia, we received word from a wealthy Muslim man I had led to Jesus just a few months prior. He told me that he had bought a high-end luxury apartment as an investment, and the construction was almost complete. He said that we could move in, rent-free, and stay there as long as we desired. Hallelujah! God wonderfully answered our prayer! When we returned, friends helped us pack and move.

It's a fascinating story of how I met this wealthy Muslim man. A friend and Chinese Christian businessman invited me to a charity golf tournament. Occasionally, I received these invitations. My Malaysian friends knew I had a gift to lead people of other faiths to Jesus. Their motive was for me to evangelize their Muslim, Buddhist, and Hindu friends and acquaintances. My friends always paid for all my expenses, making it easy to accept their invitations.

After we golfed, everyone proceeded to a banquet room to eat and hear a guest speaker share the Gospel. As I scanned the banquet room for a place to sit, I saw a group of men sitting in the back, smoking cigarettes, and drinking beer. I smiled and said to myself, "That's the perfect place for me to sit."

Arriving at their table, I introduced myself and asked permission to sit. The men cautiously looked me over and said, "Sure, please join us." Curiously, they asked where I was from and doing in Malaysia. Oh, those are priceless questions - that's all I needed to share the "Good News" of salvation with these men. I was overcome with joy, knowing God had led me to them. Those are the moments when the unction of the Holy Spirit comes on me with a burning passion. I could not keep silent and was resolved to share Jesus and reveal God's glory!

With exuberance, I shared my love for Jesus, what He had done for me, and that He sent my wife and me to Malaysia to reveal His love to anyone who would listen. Passionately, I shared many testimonies of how God used us to bless Muslims, Buddhists, and Hindus in Malaysia. I poured out my heart! My boldness, conviction, and testimonies captivated their attention.

One of the men, a wealthy Muslim businessman, asked for my phone number. Later that day, he called and asked if he could send his chauffeur to bring me to his home to learn more about Jesus. I enthusiastically agreed.

His house was large and beautiful. After I sat down, this humble Muslim man sat at my feet. With tears streaming down his face, he said, "I believe what you said about Jesus and God's plan for salvation to be true. I want Jesus to be my Lord and Savior. Will you help me to make that so?" I replied, "Of course, but please don't sit at my feet. I'm a man just like you in need of God's grace." He refused to move and asked me to pray for him. As I led him in a prayer of surrender, he joyfully wept.

He then asked if I could secretly bring him a Bible and a cross necklace. He told me that his wife would undoubtedly report him to the religious police if she discovered he had converted to Christianity. She was a proud woman who enjoyed the pleasures of high society and would not allow anything to take that away. He told me he needed time to work out how he would share his new faith with his wife. In the meantime, he told me he would keep his Bible hidden. He wanted to wear a cross necklace hidden under his clothes always to remind him he belonged to Jesus.

We lived in his luxury apartment for six months while renovating a house we bought. While living there, we conducted weekly Bible studies for new disciples. We also used the swimming pool to baptize new Believers. God works all things together for those who love and trust Him!

And the scribes of the Pharisees, when they saw that he was eating with sinners and tax collectors, said to his disciples, "Why does he eat with tax collectors and sinners?" And when Jesus heard it, he said to them, "Those who are well have no need of a physician, but those who are sick. I came not to call the righteous, but sinners,"
(Mark 2:16-17 - ESV).

Reflections—

It's amazing how God works ALL things together for those who love and trust Him (see Romans 8:28). Often, we allow unexpected and undesirable events to preoccupy our thoughts with worry. I admit, often I have thought, "I didn't see this coming. This is not going to turn out well."

Gratefully, Jesus knows our weaknesses. Jesus gave up His divine privileges to become a man and experience everything we do. So we can confidently put our trust in His empathy.

God's Word is powerful and will always bring success when we believe and obey. His Word encourages us to not worry about anything, even when confronted with overwhelming troubles. When wrestling with worry, God instructs us to make our supplications known to Him, always thanking Him for a good outcome. Those declarations of faith move mountains. Jesus showed us it's possible to remain in divine peace amid our storms.

I have experienced indescribable suffering often in my life, physically, emotionally, and relationally. At times, I have been so stricken with hurt or despair, I have stayed up all night with Jesus until God's perfect peace broke through. Amid my battles, I have learned to run to God. He alone is my refuge and salvation. In God's presence, my false imaginations and worry flee. Moreover, I am overcome by His amazing grace, peace, joy, and love (see Psalms 46:10).God takes great pleasure eradicating our sorrow and overcoming us with joy (see Jeremiah 31:13).

God sent us to be missionaries at an older age than most. That came with many advantages. One, we had learned how to deal with heartbreaking trials and troubles. When our landlord gave us an eviction notice, we trusted God would provide another place. Magnificently, God poured out His goodness beyond our expectations; we were given a luxury apartment free of rent.

Whenever you feel surrounded by trouble, do not listen to the voice of worry or despair; their purpose is to lock you up in a cell of misery. God not only loves you, but He deeply cares for you. God wants to be intimate with every detail of your life, no matter how small. God is forever faithful and good, even when we are not. In Jesus, we can always trust God!

Trust in the LORD with all your heart, and do not lean on your own understanding. In all your ways acknowledge him, and he will make straight your paths (Proverbs 3:5-6 - NLT).

Paralyzed Boy in a Wheelchair
is Miraculously Healed

God called us to Malaysia to bring the gospel of salvation primarily to Muslims, which required most of our time, energy, and resources. Occasionally, we received invitations from Malaysian Chinese and Indian Christian leaders to conduct revival/healing meetings in their communities. We accepted a few invitations when compelled by the Holy Spirit. Besides, we loved the Buddhist and Hindu communities, and many found salvation and healings at our events.

One such invitation was with a church we had befriended, primarily Chinese. They have three campuses in different cities, one located in Taiping, Malaysia. The leaders saw God had given us unusual grace to evangelize those of other faiths and ethnic backgrounds. So they were excited and hopeful for us to conduct a revival/healing service in their city.

They expected a sizeable turnout and rented a large banquet room in an exquisite hotel. They sent invitations to everyone they knew, primarily Buddhist friends, family, and acquaintances.

Immediately upon arriving, a Christian Indian doctor approached us with an Indian family. They arrived early, hoping we would pray for their son before our meeting started. We knew the doctor; he was chief of surgery at a local hospital. The doctor and his family attended the Chinese church we had befriended.

I asked them how we could pray. The doctor wept bitterly and replied, "My tragic mistake caused this boy (Daniel) to be paralyzed. It's bad enough he will never walk again, but my mistake also caused him to bear chronic severe pain. Only a miracle can save him now. I can do nothing more."

Grief-stricken, we and our team wept! Seeing this young boy winching in excruciating pain was gut-wrenching.

With tears flowing down our cheeks, we cried out for Jesus to do a miracle. We prayed, cried, and prayed more. But nothing happened! No improvement! Since the revival meeting was about to start and packed, we told the family we would pray again for Daniel after our meeting. Still hoping for a miracle, they patiently waited.

Most present were love-starved, hoping to receive a heavenly touch. The world is hungry for righteousness and salvation. And the world does not know where to find it until somebody introduces Jesus. After preaching a message about Jesus and His crucifixion, I invited those who wanted prayer to come forward. Multitudes came upfront to receive prayers for salvation, healing, guidance, and other requests. While ministering, I found it difficult to focus; I kept thinking about Daniel and his family. I was eager to pray for him again.

The Indian family was still patiently waiting after everyone had left. Hence, we could focus our full attention on Daniel. After travailing in prayer and still seeing no improvement, I sought God for guidance.

Compelled by the Holy Spirit, I knelt in front of Daniel and compassionately into his eyes. Tenderly, I said, "Jesus is going to meet you privately and heal you." I wrestle, giving prophetic words to anyone. I'm fearful of providing false hope, but a strong unction of the Holy Spirit prompted me to declare that prophetic word. It was a difficult departure; we left feeling defeated and miserable.

Six months later, Kathy and I were ministering at the Chinese church that sponsored the revival meeting. After I preached, I conducted an altar call, as I always do. And like most of our meetings, everyone came forward for prayer.

While I was praying for a person, Kathy came running to me - she was hysterical with joy. She said, "Mark, Mark, Mark, you must come with me now." Kathy apologized to the person I was praying for, grabbed my arm, and led me to a teenage Indian boy and his family. Then Kathy said gleefully, "Mark, do you recognize this boy?" I racked my brain and replied, "Sorry, I don't remember him." Overwhelmed with joy, Kathy shouted, "This is Daniel, the paralyzed boy we prayed for six months ago. Jesus met him privately and healed him, just like you prophesized!" The boy stood with a grin that stretched from ear to ear. His family stood by eager to share their victory in Jesus!

God is faithful! God is good! All glory to King Jesus! Never give up in prayer! Never throw away your confidence in Jesus! Patiently endure with a heart of thanksgiving and continue to pray until you get the promise of your hope!

Though I was uncertain about releasing a prophetic word over the paralyzed boy, I'm glad I did. God watched over His Word, and it did not come back void but fulfilled its purpose.

For as the rain and the snow come down from heaven and do not return there but water the earth, making it bring forth and sprout, giving seed to the sower and bread to the eater,

so shall my word be that goes out from my mouth; it shall not return to me empty, but it shall accomplish that which I purpose, and shall succeed in the thing for which I sent it (Isaiah 55:10-11 - ESV).

Reflections

Jesus tells us if our prayers aren't answered, to keep praying until they are. To illustrate His point, Jesus told a parable about a woman who sought justice from an uncaring judge. She hounded the judge until he relented and gave her justice. In contrast, when we seek justice from our Heavenly Father, He will do so with much pleasure, not begrudgingly (see Luke 18:1-8). But we must believe, and not doubt, to receive (see Matthew 12:21-22).

By Jesus' stripes, the legal right for Daniel's healing was already accomplished (see Isaiah 53:5). Jesus paid fully for Daniel's restoration at the 'whipping post.' That is a kingdom truth! However, there is a chasm between Christ's kingdom and our earthly reality. Heavenly blessings will only cross through that chasm and bring healing through faith-filled prayers. That's why Jesus commands us to pray: "Your kingdom come, your will be done on earth as it is in heaven" (Matthew 6:10 NLT). And we know there is no illness or injury in heaven.

Everyone Jesus prayed for was healed, even the ungrateful (see Matthew 4:23 & 11:20). Jesus gave us authority over all disease and evil spirits (Mark 16:17-18). Kathy and I have seen thousands of miraculous healings over the years, including a person raised from the dead. I don't know why Daniel did not receive his healing immediately. I'm grateful we did not give up in prayer until he was.

I have been healed of three incurable infirmities. When I was younger, I had a rare type of arthritis. The pain was chronic and severe. My doctors told me there was no cure; I would have to remain on high doses of methotrexate and prednisone for the rest of my life. My arthritis attacked all my joints, my eyes, and my heart. Over time, I lost all faith in a miracle. I am so grateful for Kathy; she persevered in faith-filled prayers for five years, never surrendering her faith in Jesus. Then suddenly, my miraculous healing came.

I will never forget that glorious morning. Like all other days, I was bearing excruciating pain. Then Jesus spoke, "Mark, I have answered Kathy's prayers; her faith has made you well." In a microsecond, my entire body was made well. Hopefully, I will be writing another book just on miraculous healings.

If you, or someone you know, needs miraculous healing, put your confidence in Jesus. And don't give up until your prayers are answered. If you are struggling with doubt, ask Jesus to help you remove your unbelief (see Mark 9:24).

Vision of an Orange Building Brings Salvation

It was always a pleasure when friends from Minnesota visited us in Malaysia. On one occasion, a married couple from Minnesota came for a friendly visit and to accompany us on evangelical outreaches to several Malaysian villages and cities. We were excited to have them meet some of our disciples and experience how we shared our faith with staunch Muslims in their communities.

Before our friends came to Malaysia, I had asked God to show our friends how He worked through us to bring salvation to Muslims. It's one thing to hear testimonies; it's another to experience them. What they witnessed would be a powerful testimony for all our friends and supporters back in Minnesota.

Early one morning, we gathered with our friends to seek God's guidance for that day. The Holy Spirit gave me a vision and another to one of our friends. Together, those visions partially revealed God's plans. I saw a road that led to a National Park. We had never been on that road, but it intersected with a highway we traveled often. Our friend saw an orange building in her vision. God spoke to me and said we would find a Muslim family who lived by an orange building located on the road to the National Park. God informed us the family was destitute and needed help; they had no food or money.

Obeying God, we bought lots of groceries and other necessities and embarked on another journey of faith. We don't always see or hear God clearly; it does not matter. If we proceed in humility and express our faith through compassion, God will be with us and cover our missteps. However, this vision was God-given; it led to numerous amazing and troubling testimonies, including salvations, divine healings, betrayals, death threats, and being investigated by the Islamic Religious Police.

We turned onto the road to the National Park, hoping to find an orange building as seen in our vision. Wonderfully, 15 miles from the intersection, we saw an orange building nestled in the jungle just past a small rural village. Close by the orange building, a Muslim family stood in front of their dilapidated house as if they were waiting for someone. There was no doubt God led us to this place.

We drove down a muddy driveway and parked our car while this family watched with suspicion and curiosity. The father's name is Mohamed, and the mother's name is Aatifa. Since white people never go into this region, they engaged cautiously. After greetings, we told them we were Christians and that our God guided us to their home through a vision, which we described. We told them our God loves them deeply and wants to bless them. They were amazed and encouraged by our testimony.

It was the God of Christians who heard their cry for help. Moreover, while their Muslim community ignored their trouble, Christians brought lifesaving relief. They were astounded and full of gratitude. God-given visions can be the seeds for a harvest of righteousness.

Trusting our intentions, Mohamed and Aatifa shared their trials and troubles with tears and trembling. They were overcome with thankfulness for all the provisions we brought. We shared Jesus and His plan for salvation and confirmed over and over that it was Jesus who sent us to their home. Our vision, generosity, and compassion opened their hearts to hear our words about Jesus and His plan for salvation.God's kindness leads people to repentance (see Romans 2:4).

Over the next few months, we visited this family often. Wonderfully, they accepted us as family. We slept in their house and did life with them, including swimming in jungle rivers, going on picnics, and helping them with daily chores. Moreover, I raised funds to help restore their home, including constructing a front porch. I also raised funds to help them grow corn and spices. Over time, our relationships with this family deepened. We also developed friendships with others in their village.

On one occasion, while visiting Mohamed and Aatifa, a young woman (Faiza) abruptly marched into their house without knocking. Apparently, she knew the family, and it was evident she wasn't happy with our presence. Faiza was an Islamic teacher, and her husband was the town mayor. She heard that Christians were evangelizing in her community. Hence, she came to investigate the claims, gather evidence, and report us to the Islamic authorities. However, God had other plans!

After befriending us, Faiza confessed her initial motive was to have us arrested and jailed. However, she couldn't follow through because she had grown fond of us. Conflicted, Faiza decided to convert us to Islam rather than report us to the religious police.

In her attempts to convert us, we politely listened as Faiza shared the virtues of Islam. Careful that our conversation didn't become a debate and argumentative, I shared the virtues of being a Christian, with the utmost reverence for Jesus. It's not wise or honorable to disparage someone else's beliefs. Instead of telling them what's wrong with their faith, I simply share mine, always doing so with patience and gentleness. I trust the Holy Spirit to reveal deception and convict hearts with the truth. We have led multitudes from other faiths using these spiritual principles.

Any hint of arrogance will close hearts when witnessing, but honor and respect are powerful virtues that open hearts. We strive not to appear superior or speak any disparaging remarks about their beliefs. It's a delicate dance to show honor to those of other faiths without compromising our beliefs. Gratefully, the Holy Spirit always guides us with revelation and wisdom.

Faiza was overtaken by our gentle, compassionate demeanor and convicted by our testimonies and teachings. Shortly later, Faiza became a Believer! That was a glorious moment. However, that was also the onset of grave trouble.

I received a phone call from Faiza; she was wailing and could barely talk. She said that someone informed her husband, the mayor, Christians were evangelizing in his village. Outraged, he organized an emergency town meeting to discuss the matter. Over two hundred people came, which was most the village. Kathy and I were the topics of discussion.

The mayor's conclusion, along with the majority, was to report us to the State Islamic Police, and they did. Hence, the police came to investigate our evangelical efforts, which brought a caning and prison sentence if found guilty. After questioning many villagers, the religious police gave them instructions to immediately report us when we returned. And they would send officers to arrest us immediately. This was not our first encounter of this nature; we weren't surprised.

We prayed with Faiza and told her we would call again after seeking God's guidance about returning or not.

Kathy and I tell everyone that Jesus lives in our hearts. And that He is perfect love, and there is no fear in love. We concluded it would be a powerful testimony of God's love if we returned to this village and faced their threats. We prepared ourselves to be arrested, jailed, and punished. That was no easy task. We initially wrestled with much fear; however, after fervent prayer, God gave us peace that surpassed all our doubts and uncertainties. God also strengthened our spirits and gave us a fresh spirit of boldness.

A couple days later, we called Faiza and told her we would be returning to her village the next day. Faiza screamed, "No, please do not come! The religious police will come and arrest you! Besides, I don't want to get into trouble being seen with you!" We empathized with her fears but really wanted to see her. So, I asked, "Are you willing to meet us in a nearby village." She agreed.

Not deterred by the threats, Mohamed and Aatifa desperately wanted to see us and did not care if it brought trouble. They were ecstatic - we felt the same way. Encouraged by their love for us, we made plans to visit them after meeting Faiza.

After an eight-hour drive, we met with Faiza in a nearby village as we planned. She was a wreck; fear and despair consumed her. We patiently and gently listened to her concerns. And we loved her and prayed God would give her peace. Sadly, Faiza continued to bemoan our fate if we returned to her village.

After meeting with Faiza, we precariously drove through Mohamed and Aatifa's village; they lived a few miles in a forested area on the other side. Many curious eyes watched as we drove by. We had become well known and they were alarmed by our return. Most had been at the infamous town meeting discussing our fate.

It was an awkward and emotional meeting with Mohamed and Aatifa. They were present at the town meeting and outraged by the proceedings. Their testimony of what happened both alarmed us and brought us to tears.

Aatifa recanted, "At the meeting, and with everyone watching, the mayor abruptly approached us. Angrily, he pointed his finger at us and shouted, 'I heard that you and your household have converted to Christianity. Is that true?'" "How did you respond? I asked." Aatifa answered, "I stood and shouted for all present to hear, 'You all know we were going through many trials and were suffering. Yet not one of you lifted a finger to help us even though you knew we had no food. In my opinion, Christians are better than Muslims.' I then sat down."

I acknowledged Aatifa's courage but added it would be best not to make disparaging remarks. I asked Aatifa how her neighbors responded to her rebuke. She said they sat in shame and silence. We were amazed by Aatifa's boldness and courage. Yet, we remained alert to danger.

We stayed with our friends that night, praying and hoping no one would report us to the State Religious Police. Gratefully, they did not come, and their neighbors gave us no trouble. Moreover, God made a way to restore favor with the village. Mohamed and Aatifa's oldest daughter were engaged. It's customary for the bride's parents to host the wedding ceremony. It's also traditional for the bride's family to slaughter and prepare a cow for all the guests to eat. However, Mohamed and Aatifa were too poor to buy a cow, so we did on their behalf. Not to bring embarrassment to our friends, we didn't want anyone in the village to know we had bought the cow. However, Aatifa proudly told everyone of our generosity.

Kathy and I were the guests of honor. Upon arrival on the wedding day, all the villagers welcomed us with much affection. I could not stop smiling, thinking about God's unfailing favor. For many years we continued to visit that village.

When facing threats, we saw them as impending assaults against Christ's gospel. We are grateful, God gave us the boldness to brush aside the imminent danger and return to the village. ALL glory to God!

"And now, O Lord, hear their threats, and give us, your servants, great boldness in preaching your word. Stretch out your hand with healing power; may miraculous signs and wonders be done through the name of your holy servant Jesus." After this prayer, the meeting place shook, and they were all filled with the Holy Spirit. Then they preached the word of God with boldness (Acts 4:29-31 - NLT)

Reflections

Satan will always strive to pervert God's will. One of his tactics is to bring fear of persecution or death. However, Jesus said, *"Don't be afraid of those who want to kill your body; they cannot touch your soul. Fear only God, who can destroy both soul and body in hell" (Matthew 10:28 - NLT).*

People have said to us, "Don't worry about someone killing you on the mission field; God will never allow that to happen." I know they mean well, but that isn't biblical. Nor is it a historical fact for missionaries. Ten of Jesus' twelve original disciples were martyred for their faith. And tens of thousands have been martyred over the centuries.

Moreover, I have been told many times by well-meaning friends, "Mark, you know Jesus tells us to be wise and careful." They really mean that we take a risk assessment before engaging in our assignments. And if it appears to be too dangerous, not to go. My response is, "I seek God for guidance and obey what He shows me, no matter the risks. That's my type of wisdom."

Before moving to Malaysia, we believed we might be martyred for our faith in fulfilling God's calling. Amid the possibility of being martyred, finding peace was difficult but necessary. Danger followed us daily, and if we surrendered to fear, we would have lost countless opportunities to glorify God. Gratefully, God granted us boldness to accomplish His will. Wonderfully, even hardcore Muslims who knew us were deeply moved by the peace and joy we beheld amid threats.

Most of the villagers in Mohamed's and Aatifa's town quietly examined our demeanor when we returned. They respected us for not bowing to their mayor's threats. Gratefully, no one reported us to the religious police.

Don't let intimidation hold you back if God has called you to say or do something. Don't let Satan rob you of advancing God's kingdom. Ask God to help you overcome your fears. And seek His goodness until His love melts away all your worries. Heavenly Father takes great pleasure in giving you perfect peace. For those who love and trust Jesus, they will do great exploits. Let it be so for you!

Muslim Woman Receives a Miraculous Healing Then Reports Us to the Police!

This story is about Faiza's mother, Rebekah. Faiza is the Islamic teacher whom I wrote about in my previous story.

Complying to Jesus' instructions (read Luke 10:1-7), when visiting a village, we only stayed at one home and one that was worthy of God's peace. On one occasion, we made the mistake of staying at more than one, which led to bitter jealousy and fighting among several families. While visiting Mohamed and Aatifa's village, whom I wrote about in my previous story, we stayed at their house.

On one occasion, early in the morning, while Mohamed and Aatifa, I heard a loud unceasing pounding on the front door. Obviously, someone was desperate! Curiously, I opened the door to see who might be troubled. We had become family with Mohamed and Aatifa, so they felt comfortable allowing us to greet visitors. To show us honor, they eagerly encouraged us to do so.

It was Faiza knocking on the door. She would have barged in, but the door was locked. Faiza was hysterical. She appeared as if someone had just died! I asked her, "Faiza, you look like you haven't slept all night; why are you so downcast." She retorted, "My mother (Rebekah) is in a terrible condition and might be close to death." "We will go immediately and pray for her, I responded." Frightened by my offer, Faiza stated, "My brother and sister are there, and they will strongly object to Christians praying for mother."

Though Faiza would not admit it, I knew she believed we were in a relationship with the true God. So, I said, "Faiza, would you rather have your mom die because you fear your sibling's rebuke?" Faiza saw the irony in the situation and relented. We all hurried over to her mother's house.

After introductions and a short gospel presentation, we prayed for Rebekah. Immediately after our prayer, Rebekah rejoiced, "I feel much better, I feel great." We all celebrated her victory! Wanting to give glory to God, I encouraged them to thank Jesus. However, I sensed Faiza's family remained suspicious of our motives. We have had several encounters in which Jesus healed those of other faiths, but they refused to give God glory. They justified their healing by believing we were witch doctors. The practice of witchcraft in Malaysia predates the beginnings of Islam. Sadly, it did not bode well for them later.

After further fellowship and prayer, Kathy and I returned to our home in Cheras, Malaysia, an eight-hour drive. As soon as we reached our house, I received a disturbing text message from Faiza that left us confused and distressed!

Faiza informed us her mother's condition went horribly wrong right after we departed. Frightened, Faiza called for an ambulance. And Rebekah was rushed to a hospital located about an hour's drive away in a large city.

After taking some tests, the doctor told Faiza and her siblings that there was nothing he could do to save their mother and that she would undoubtedly die within three days. Subsequently, the doctor advised Faiza to immediately inform all her family members so they would have enough time to come and say their goodbyes.

In her phone text, Faiza stated that her siblings, who were present when we prayed for their mother, informed the entire family that 'white witch doctors' put a death curse on their mother. Consequently, the whole family was furious with us. Moreover, Faiza stated one of her brothers, who lived in a different city, was a police officer. She feared he would have us arrested. This was not the report we were expecting.

Shocked and confused, Kathy and I prayed, "Lord, what would you have us do now?" We trusted Jesus had a plan and remained in control, despite the dire circumstances. Jesus is God; therefore, nothing is a surprise to Him. And He always has a plan!

Jesus answered, "Pray for a 'special gift' of faith (see 1 Corinthians 12:9); buy a plane ticket to the city where Rebekah is hospitalized and leave tomorrow morning. Once at the hospital, immediately pray for Rebekah, and I will heal her." I thought to myself, "Did I hear correctly or was it a false imagination." Then I remembered the scripture from the Book of James:

If you need wisdom, ask our generous God, and he will give it to you. He will not rebuke you for asking. But when you ask him, be sure that your faith is in God alone. Do not waver, for a person with divided loyalty is as unsettled as a wave of the sea that is blown and tossed by the wind (James 1:5-6 NLT).

Trusting we heard God, we bought a plane ticket and left early the following day. Upon arrival, the hospital receptionist informed us we would find Faiza and her family at the hospital's far end. That was an awkward moment. Rebekah was hospitalized in a region that strongly opposed Christians. Moreover, the hospital had no private rooms; all the patients were in beds in large open spaces. As we walked the entire length of the room, multitudes of Muslims suspiciously glared at us; our knees were knocking.

I whispered to Kathy, "Just keep smiling. When we get to Faiza's family, don't engage in small talk. They will strongly oppose our prayers because they believe we are 'white witch doctors.' Let's trust we heard correctly from Jesus, and when we arrive, immediately lay your hands on Rebekah and pray."

As we were approached Faiza's family, they all shrank back in fright by our presence. Probably, because they feared we might release a deadly curse on them. However, their trepidation worked to our advantage. It allowed Kathy to pray unhindered.

Kathy swiftly placed her hands on Rebekah and prayed without any interference or objections from her family. Jesus miraculously and swiftly rewarded our faithful obedience by immediately healing Rebekah. She cried out, "I felt a current of power run through my entire body. I know I am healed."

The family immediately summoned her doctor. He quickly came, carefully listened to Rebekah, took some tests, and confirmed that she was completely healed. It was an amazing miracle in the presence of multitudes! Everyone rejoiced! Gratefully, we could relax.

We told Faiza's family how Jesus gave us instructions not to throw away our confidence in Him but persevere in faith until Rebekah received healing. They were astonished. They knew we put our lives in danger in hopes Rebekah got healed. Wonderfully, their attitude towards us swiftly improved from contempt to respect and honor.

Faiza's brother, the police officer, bought us a meal later that day at a nearby restaurant. It was a marvelous celebration. But, sadly, our friendship with Rebekah went horribly sour in the coming months.

Encouraged by the miraculous healing, Faiza, Rebekah, and two of Faiza's siblings surrendered their lives to Jesus. We brought them to an island resort off the East Coast of Malaysia for three days of intense discipleship. In a secluded environment, they would not have to worry about being exposed and persecuted. At the resort, we gave them Bibles, and other Christian material, which is illegal.

When teaching new Believers, I begin with the 'Beatitudes' and other lessons from the 'Sermon on the Mount.' They are beautiful instructions about being happy and prosperous in Christ's kingdom as God's children. Whoever commits to growing in these divine truths will enjoy a virtuous, joyful, and productive life in Christ Jesus.

Also, in those lessons, I teach about the dangers of bitterness and the power of forgiveness. I asked Rebekah to make a list of all those who she has not forgiven. Rebekah became bitter and would not comply. She mocked the teaching about forgiveness and said, "I hate Mohamed and Aatifa. When they die, I will spit on their grave." She went on, "And I know you stay at their house when you visit my village. If you continue to do so, I will make trouble for you." No matter how much we tried to convince her otherwise, Rebekah would not budge.

Giving her grace and patience, we visited Rebekah a couple more times. She was unappreciative and remained bitter. She allowed us to come to her house, hoping we would give her money or other items. We did not! Her rebellion deemed her unworthy to keep God's peace (see Matthew 10:13). Our time with Rebekah was unfruitful, so we decided our time was more productive visiting others in her village.

Two months later, we received a phone call from Faiza. She was crying hysterically. Faiza said, "My mother has reported you guys to the village mayor, my husband. And she gave him the Bibles and other Christian material you gave her. My husband, in return, has reported you to the State Religious Police. They are going to come and investigate the claims. You guys are in danger of being imprisoned." I shared in my previous story what happened afterward.

"Love your enemies! Do good to them. Lend to them without expecting to be repaid. Then your reward from heaven will be very great, and you will truly be acting as children of the Most High, for he is kind to those who are unthankful and wicked. You must be compassionate, just as your Father is compassionate" (Luke 6:35-36 - NLT).

Reflections

Not everyone honored God, who Jesus healed. Jesus denounced three cities that rejected Him. And those were cities in which Jesus performed most of His miracles (see Matthew 11:20). Additionally, Jesus healed ten lepers; only one praised God and thanked Him (see Luke 17:12-14).

The same has happened to us; we have prayed for those who were miraculously healed, and they refused to praise God. On one occasion, I prayed for a Somali man who had immense pain in his leg. Jesus healed him. Though I made it very clear that Jesus, the Son of God, healed him, he gave thanks to Allah. Sadly, the Somali man had no interest in hearing the Good News. He abruptly walked away, just like the ungrateful nine lepers who Jesus healed.

Rebekah was ungrateful for her healing. She believed our testimony about Jesus but refused to be His "Follower." There is a vital difference between believing who Jesus is and being His disciple. Even Satan believes Jesus is the Son of God. Rebekah wanted to have a relationship with Jesus on her terms, not God's. Forgiving those who hate, harm, curse, and oppose us is not optional; it is a commandment from God (see Matthew 6:14).

Nevertheless, even though Rebekah remained bitter, we accomplished much for God's glory. Her whole family witnessed her miraculous healing. Moreover, Rebekah's testimony spread throughout her village. That, undoubtedly, gave us much favor to preach God's word in their midst.

I always ask the Holy Spirit to reveal any grudges, contempt, anger, complaints, or judgments I might have towards others. Resurrection power for eternal salvation and earthly restoration is only available to those who abide in a spirit of forgiveness. I earnestly strive to love, pray, do good things, and bless my enemies. When compassion for my enemies replaces all contempt, I know I have totally forgiven them (see Luke 6:27-36).

Memories of injustice will always remain, but the pain from those memories can be totally healed. If memories continue to torment you, I encourage you to ask God to help you forgive. Perhaps you forgave but then returned to unforgiveness. Complete inner-healing for past hurts will only come when you have fully forgiven. God loves you deeply and wants you to be free!

Detained by the Police
for Preaching Jesus

We brought three of our spiritual sons (former Muslims) to a pictur-esque Islamic city nestled beside the South China Sea for the pur-pose of evangelism. A pristine beach, tall palm trees, and a deep blue ocean presented a scenic backdrop for our day of ministry. We were excited and expectant God was going to reveal His glory. By our example, we had shown our sons how to share the gospel with power. This day was their opportunity to demonstrate what they learned by taking the lead.

As we entered this Malaysian city, hundreds of locals lined both sides of the main road. They were selling produce, chickens, goats, fish, clothing, and other items. It was market day, so there would be ample opportunity for ministry. It was also Ramadan, the Muslims Holy month. From sunrise to sunset, Muslims fast from food and drink.

Our sons were confident and eager because they had seen God perform miraculous healings, deliverances, salvations, and other signs and wonders through our ministry. However, evangelizing Muslims is illegal, so it was difficult to completely rid ourselves of all apprehension. We constantly fought off thoughts of being arrested and persecuted. In those moments, God always gave us peace and passion. God's grace always triumphed over our fears so that we could accomplish our assignments.

After we arrived in the marketplace, the Holy Spirit prompted our sons to engage with an elderly Muslim woman sitting on a small wooden box. She was selling produce. After sharing their testimony about Jesus, they offered prayers for healing; she commented that she suffered from chronic leg pain and welcomed prayer. Many marketplace merchants curiously watched as our sons prayed for the elderly lady to be healed. Wonderfully, Jesus healed her. Shocked, the elderly woman stood, raised her hands to the sky, and praised Jesus. It was a fantastic start to a brilliant day. But our mission work never went smoothly. Later that day, we encountered a challenging trial.

We continued to freely minister in the marketplace with no one taking offense. I prayed for a man who had difficulty breathing; he was asthmatic. Jesus healed him. Breathing much better and full of gratitude, he thanked Jesus. We had delightful conversations with many merchants that day, always mentioning, "God Jesus sent us to reveal His love and blessings!"After a few hours of marketplace ministry, my eyes were drawn to a large Mosque about a block from us. It was more than curiosity; Holy Spirit compelled me to go there. God said, "Mark, I want you to take your team across the street and minister to the people working in the Mosque compound." My team nervously agreed to go. Numerous women were preparing food in huge pots for a feast that evening. As I mentioned, Muslims fast from sunrise to sunset during their Holy month, Ramadan.

Once we arrived, I noticed an Imam (Muslim priest) standing close by the compound's wall. I asked him if we could enter. He allowed us with one condition; Kathy had to wear a 'tudung' (head-covering for women). Respecting their culture, Kathy complied.

Once in the compound area, the Holy Spirit prompted me to share the gospel of salvation with all the women workers but start with Abraham and work my way forward to Jesus. Muslims believe in Abraham, Moses, and many other people in the Bible. Thus, it was wise to start my preaching at a place they had an understanding and would not object to.

Whenever God honors me with an opportunity to share Jesus and His plan for salvation, I am overcome with joy, no matter the circumstances. Moreover, it is with much gratitude I preach because of what Jesus has done in my life. At the end of my message, I boldly told the women, "Jesus is our Healer, and He wants to heal you today. Is there anyone who would like prayer?"

A dignified woman who appeared to be captivated by my sermon grabbed Kathy's arm and took her to the mosque's front steps for prayer. God had granted her faith to believe. She asked Kathy to sit with her on the Mosque steps and pray for Jesus to heal her chronic back pain. With multitudes watching, Kathy placed her hands on the woman's back and prayed. Amazingly, Jesus instantly healed her! The Muslim woman stood, and with a broad smile, praised Jesus! It was a glorious moment we will never forget.

Sadly, not everyone present was happy about her healing or my preaching. Several Imams were watching our every move; their faces grimaced with disapproval and anger. It was an awkward moment; maleficence stirred in their hearts. Our subsequent actions only exacerbated the situation.

Not much later, the local men were entering the Mosque for prayer, and our spiritual sons wanted to join them. They said, "Dad, let's go into the Mosque and quietly worship Jesus. We can pray God gives everyone a revelation about who Jesus is." Always looking for a new adventure, I replied, "Okay, let's go."

In the Mosque, a man asked me, "Are you a Muslim?" He was suspicious and annoyed by my presence. Confidently, I replied, "No, I am a Christian pastor. If I am not welcome here, I will leave. People of all faiths are welcome in my church, but I appreciate your customs might be different." He did not respond and moved on indignantly.

Since I was not accustomed to their worship practices, I followed one of our sons' movements. When he knelt and placed his forehead on the floor, I did the same. After what seemed like a long time with my forehead pasted to the floor, I wondered why my son remained mysteriously still. I reached over and poked him; he had fallen asleep. The other congregants were standing. We both promptly stood with guilty faces; it was embarrassing.

The Imam glared at us with disapproval and contempt. After the service, he called the police. They came and brought us to the police station. Since Kathy is a woman, she did not participate in the service and was not detained. That was a good thing; she could immediately contact our Intercessors for emergency prayer.

At the police station, we were separated and taken to different rooms for interrogation. A mean-spirited policeman interrogated me. He was very abusive. Annoyed and angry, I refused to cooperate with him. I said, "You are a bad man, and I won't talk with you. I will only talk to the chief of police." Irritated, he complied and fetched his boss, who was interrogating one of our sons in another room.

I stood squarely in front of the chief, looked intently into his eyes, and said, "Why are you arresting us; for doing kind acts? Your citizens are being healed in Jesus' name. Are we breaking the law by asking our God to heal your people?"

My tirade distressed the chief, but I sensed he was not angry. He was scared, disoriented, and struggled to respond. I asked the officer, "Are you sick or injured, or do you know someone who is? If you allow me to pray for healing, my God will do a miracle. And that will prove my God loves and cares for you."

The chief started to sweat profusely; it was apparent he was distraught. I believe he was thinking, "If I let them go, I will be in big trouble with my superiors. But, if I incarcerate them, I will be in serious trouble with their God." A quick side note. The Bible states that Jesus knew the thoughts of those who opposed Him. The Bible also says that we have the "mind of Christ" (see 1 Corinthians 2:16). Jesus is our perfect example on how to reveal God's kingdom in every circumstance.

After a few tense moments, the chief shouted, "Get out of my station! Leave before I change my mind." Relieved, we complied and swiftly departed.

When people's lives please the Lord, even their enemies
are at peace with them (Proverbs 16:7 NLT).

One year later, during Ramadan, God instructed me to return to the same police station. The Holy Spirit gave me the impression that a policeman on duty desperately needed ministry. I also felt compelled by the Holy Spirit to find the Imam, who reported us to the police.

This would be another awkward mission. Two young Malaysian men were with us when the Lord spoke to me. We were teaching them Muslim evangelism by example. After I shared God's plans to go to the police station, they raised their hands and said, "Well, it's a good day to die!" I was amused by their humor and smiled. They were brave students.

When we arrived at the police station, we were met by a policeman we had not met when I was detained the prior year. After introductions, this young policeman asked, "How can I help you?" "Our God sent us to bless you, and I believe He is telling me that you are experiencing a horrifying trial." The policeman's demeanor quickly shifted to fright. He retorted, "What is your God telling you about me?"

I responded, "Forgive me if I have not heard correctly. I believe my God is telling me that an enemy of yours paid a witch doctor to put a curse on you and your family. Consequently, you and your family have been tormented by unusual events causing much fear. Moreover, with a vengeful heart, you paid a higher-powered witch doctor to put a curse on your enemy and the witch doctor who cursed you."

The policeman's mouth dropped open, and he began to tremble in fear. He confirmed everything I said to be accurate and asked if I was a white witch doctor wanting to harm him. I assured him that my God sent us to break the curse over him and his family. I used the policeman's tormenting circumstances to introduce the 'Good News of Salvation.' Also, I described how blessings overcome and destroy curses in Jesus Christ's kingdom.

The policeman was shocked by the accuracy of my prophetic words. Also, he was profoundly convicted by the testimony of Jesus and His crucifixion. I asked the policeman if he believed everything I spoke about salvation. He did! God had removed the veil of deception that kept him blind from the truth.

Encouraged by my prompting, the policeman confessed his sins, asked for God's forgiveness, and surrendered his life to Jesus. He forgave and blessed all his enemies, including those who cursed him with a sincere heart.

I told the policeman he now belonged to Jesus, and all his sins have been forgiven. Therefore, evil no longer had the legal right to torment him and his family. He allowed me to exert my authority to break the curse, which I did in Jesus' Name.

What happened next brought us to tears. Heavenly Father graciously poured out the oil of joy on this humble policeman! Instantly, his countenance transformed from fright to ecstasy. It is impossible to conjure up that type of pleasure; it only comes from above. It was a remarkable and memorable moment. The policeman was giddy. With a broad smile, he thanked and praised Jesus for His goodness. However, our business in this Islamic city was not finished.

I asked the policeman, "Now that you are my spiritual son, could you help us on another matter? Last year, the local Imam reported us to the police; subsequently, I was detained at this station. Could you help us find him?" He eagerly complied, made some phone calls, and told us we would find the Iman at an open-air restaurant across the street from the Mosque.

When we arrived, the Imam, and his Mosque workers, were chatting while waiting for the sun to set. The Imam immediately recognized us. Shocked by our audacity to return to his city, he barked, "What is the purpose of your visit." Undeterred by his demeanor, I boldly responded, "My God has something to say to you." He replied, "And what would that be?" I responded, "I don't know; God hasn't told me yet. I will ask Him now."

Jesus instructed his disciples not to preplan what to speak when taken before authorities; the Holy Spirit would teach them that hour what to say (see Luke 12:11-12).

Sometimes, the Holy Spirit gives me His entire narrative. Other times, He gives me portion by portion. The latter was the case this day. What I first heard from the Holy Spirit frightened me. I thought to myself, "If I share this word, we could be in big trouble. Nevertheless, God's thoughts and ways are far above ours."

Looking into the group of hard-core Muslims, I declared, "Jesus sent my wife and me to Malaysia to start a revolution!" That did not go over well; the men appeared as though they would execute us immediately. The next thing the Holy Spirit instructed me to share was even more frightening.

Trusting God and not daunted by fear, I boldly spoke, "Jesus sent Kathy and me to Malaysia to overthrow the government." I was stunned by their response; the men were smiling! Later, I was informed they perceived Malaysia's ruling party to be weak. They hoped for a more conservative Islamic party to overthrow them. They sat waiting to hear more.

Gratefully, the Holy Spirit downloaded the rest of His message, and I had their full attention. With compassion and conviction, I declared, "God did not send us to Malaysia to start a revolution of the land or overthrow the Malaysian government. God sent us to initiate a revolution in people's hearts—hearts ruled by darkness. God wants me to tell you about His kingdom of light and His Son, whom He sent as light to shine into the darkness. Captivated by my words, they eagerly listened.

I shared about God's kingdom of righteousness, holiness, and compassion. And with tears streaming down my cheeks, I shared my testimony. I will never hide my reverence and love for Jesus, no matter the cost. I could see in their eyes they were profoundly moved and convicted by my testimony. Moreover, they respected my boldness in the face of probable persecution.

The Imam, who detained us the prior year, spoke, "Now that I know your heart, you are free to do mission work in my city." What extraordinary favor God gave us! Another hard-core Islamic leader welcomed us to his city.

One of the Imam's workers lifted his garment and asked for prayers for his injured leg. The Holy Spirit had given a team member of ours a prophetic vision of this man. So, he prayed for him.

For a season, whenever we were in that region, we stopped to buy groceries and necessities for the poor from the Imam; he owned a grocery store across the street from his Mosque. Though he never gave his life to Jesus (that we know of), this Imam became our ministry partner in that region.

Things are not always as they appear. When we keep our confidence in Jesus, God is able and willing to perform extraordinary miracles despite dire and uncertain circumstances.

Some Jews arrested me in the Temple for preaching this, and they tried to kill me. But God has protected me right up to this present time so I can testify to everyone, from the least to the greatest. I teach nothing except what the prophets and Moses said would happen—that the Messiah would suffer and be the first to rise from the dead, and in this way announce God's light to Jews and Gentiles alike,"
(Acts 26:21-23 - NLT).

Reflections

God instructs us always to be ready to preach His Word, in season or out of season (see 2 Timothy 4:2). It was dangerous for Moses to confront Pharaoh. The same was true with Daniel, Esther, Peter, Paul, and many other biblical figures chosen by God to confront authorities who could have them killed. They believed and obeyed God. Consequently, their obedience changed the world.

God turned for good what the Imam meant for harm. After being detained, God instructed us to return to the Imam's city. Not knowing God's purpose, we obeyed. Consequently, a policeman found salvation, and the Imam and his Mosque subordinates heard the Good News with open hearts. This was not a world-changing event, but all in Heaven celebrated another soul receiving eternal life.

Not everyone has the calling to be an evangelist, but everyone is called to be Christ's witness. Therefore, all Christians should always be ready to testify about their faith and love for Jesus. If you remain prepared, you might find your most powerful encounters will occur when they are least convenient.

Prophetic Vision Leads
a Muslim Clan to Jesus

Sometimes God's plans for our evangelical outreaches are revealed through visions. On one such occasion, as we were praying for God's guidance, I received a vision. The Holy Spirit showed me a road leading to a Muslim fishing village. I saw fishermen on a beach, preparing their boats and nets for their day's fishing. We had never been on the road, but it intersected with the main road we traveled often. God instructed us to go to this village nestled on the South China Sea and share His truth, love, and blessings with the fishermen.

As we drove through a port city, we detoured from the primary road onto a side road. I sensed this was the road in my vision. We proceeded down this narrow, windy, rut-filled road, which meandered between broken-down shanty houses until we came to the beach with the fishermen.

When we arrived, we were met with a magnificent vista. The sun was shining; a gentle breeze kept us cool, and tropical Islands could be seen jutting from the turquoise ocean. And the fishermen were preparing their nets and boats for a day of fishing. Just as I saw in my vision. Also, we were entertained by a monkey throwing coconuts from a coconut tree for his owner to collect for sale. It was a glorious day.

After introductions, I shared the vision God gave me with a few fishermen. I told them our God sent us to bless them. After a brief description of Jesus and His gospel, I asked if we could pray for Jesus to give them success in their efforts. Several of the fishermen allowed us to do so. I sensed they were touched by our compassionate words, testimonies, and prayers.

Two young Malaysian men accompanied us on this evangelical outreach.

We were training them in Muslim evangelism by hands-on example. One of our students brought his guitar. In the presence of all the fishermen, my team stood ankle-deep in the ocean, and we worshiped. We also anointed the sea with oil and asked God to bless the fishermen with success. Oh, what a precious moment that was!

That evening, we stayed at a motel close by. Soon after we arrived at the beach early the following morning, an elderly Muslim man (Saad) approached me; he was distraught. Saad got straight to the point and asked, "Did I hear you correctly yesterday that your God Jesus is a Healer?" There was a lot of pain in his voice. Overcome with compassion, I gently responded, "Sir, you heard correctly. What is your concern?"

Saad was a gentle and kind man. He told us that one of his grandsons recently died from a blood disease, thalassemia. And now, his brother (Anwar) was close to dying from the same condition. Saad asked if we would come to his house and pray for his grandson to be healed. This brokenhearted Muslim did not care we were Christians. He was hoping our God would heal his grandson; that's all that mattered. We graciously accepted his invitation and drove a short distance to his house.

Upon arrival, many in his clan were present. Two of the family members went into a bedroom, fetched Anwar, and carried him to the middle of the family area. He was too weak to walk or stand. Anwar was about ten years of age but looked six. Since birth, he struggled with thalassemia, which stunted his natural growth.

I shared Jesus and the gospel with all present. They listened politely. I also shared healing testimonies hoping to lift their faith, but sadness and fear consumed them. Two others in this family were struggling with the same disease. However, everyone was hoping for a miracle.Kathy and one of our team members prayed for Anwar to be healed. Miraculously, in the precious Name of Jesus, God's healing power came upon this dear child. Though Anwar did not receive complete healing, he could stand independently. He and everyone else was overcome with joy, and we all rejoiced in God's goodness. Our two students who came with us led us in worship songs in the Malay language! Since the families were Muslim, they didn't know the song's meaning but showed approval with broad smiles. It was a glorious time, and we became instant friends with a clan of seven Muslim families.

Over the next six months, we visited this clan often. During that period, seven families made decisions to convert to Christianity. Anwar and his wife (Halima) led the way. They announced to their family, "We are going to follow Mark and Kathy's faith and become Christians." Kathy and I led Anwar and Halima in a 'prayer salvation.' It was essential to Anwar and Halima that their family witness this historic event.

That opened the hearts of the clan to do the same. Over many months, one by one, the fathers would gather their families together and ask us to lead them in a prayer of salvation.

However, Saad told us that his oldest son, who we had not met, heard of their conversion, and threatened to report everyone to the religious police, including us. The families were terrified. Moreover, Saad told me their neighbors threatened to construct a blockade on the road to their house and attack us on our next visit. However, their threats did not deter us from discipling our precious family. My next story describes our encounter with Saad's oldest son, Mohamed.

We had become accustomed to such threats. We wanted Muslims to see that our love was supernatural and triumphed over fear. So, whenever our new disciples allowed us to visit, we came, despite threats of violence and death. Additionally, we wanted everyone to see we walked in peace and joy, not fear or anger. We were told later that our gentle demeanor, despite all the threats, was a powerful testimony about our faith in Jesus.

God blessed this clan with many miraculous signs and wonders for the next two years. But then, calamity sprung forth. Two family members died prematurely. And two pregnant mothers had unexpected miscarriages. Consequently, unbearable heartache and confusion overcame them. Satan exploited their misery by convincing them all their troubles were from Allah--he was punishing them for becoming Christians. Moreover, Satan enticed them to return to Islam.

It became a long, drawn-out, spiritual war. We bitterly wept through these trials but never gave up. We continued to pray for this precious clan, believing they would return to Jesus!

This family initially experienced wondrous miracles. Anwar was never fully healed, but he enjoyed life beyond expectations to his doctor's amazement. Also, Anwar received another bizarre but beautiful miracle.

Thalassemia stunted his penis from growing. Consequently, his doctor could not perform a circumcision. This brought much shame, embarrassment, and sorrow to Anwar and his parents. Circumcision had much cultural significance.

We asked Anwar and his parents for permission to pray for his penis to grow miraculously. They eagerly consented. Over the next few days, Anwar's penis grew. Encouraged by the miracle, Anwar's parents took him to the clinic. After examination, his doctor was amazed and circumcised Anwar.

We learned one of Saad's sons was severely demonized on another visit. He was a strong young man. However, an evil spirit would come on him at nighttime, causing him to terrify his family and community. After sharing some deliverance testimonies, the demonic son allowed me to cast out the evil spirit tormenting him. Gratefully, until this day, he has remained free and is known by his community to be a gentle giant.

On another occasion, a one-year-old baby boy in this clan swallowed a brass hairpin causing him to be poisoned. He became gravely ill, but, for whatever reason, his parents were too intimidated to bring him to the hospital. However, they allowed us, along with Saad, to rush their baby to a hospital two hours away. The parents had been checking their baby's poop to see if the brass hairpin had passed through, but it had not.

On the way to the hospital, we prayed Jesus would dissolve the brass hairpin and heal the baby. After examining the x-rays, the doctor stated no hairpin was present. After more tests, the doctor said there were no signs of poison. We weren't surprised. By the time we had arrived at the hospital, the baby boy was astoundingly better, so we knew God had answered our prayers. In a short time, that precious baby boy went from being violently ill to being well—all praise to Jesus, our Healer.

As I mentioned earlier, after a season of peace and joy, trouble started to rain down on this clan like a mighty storm. A young wife who was pregnant allowed us to lay our hands on her womb and pray for God's blessing over her unborn child. Soon later, her baby was stillborn. Tragically, it happened with another young mother from this clan a second time. Also, Saad asked me to pray for him; he had heart problems. One week after I laid my hands on his chest and prayed, Saad died. Then Saad's oldest son mysteriously died. I have good reason to believe he was killed for his faith in Jesus. All these tragedies happened in a short period. Those tragedies brought gut-wrenching, indescribable heartache and much confusion.

With her husband's sudden death and all the other calamities, Halima and the rest of her family became confused about Christianity. Moreover, our presence frightened them. First, they experienced many miracles. Now tragedy and misery had become their bedpartners. They told us to leave and never come back.

Kathy and I were devastated. We bitterly wept! This clan had become our family, and they had a special place in our hearts. We saw they had returned to the Islam faith on our last visit. We were devasted! However, love never quits, no matter the circumstances. Love will always pursue victory until it's solidified. God's love within us would not allow us to abandon this precious family.

For many months we beseeched God for guidance on how to bring this clan back to Jesus. When I was least expecting it, God revealed His plan. We were in a city about an hour's drive from Halima and her family, visiting another clan we had led to Jesus. A few of our mission team members, all Malaysians, accompanied us on this trip.

As we sat and talked with one another, God spoke, "Mark, what do you see?" He then opened my eyes to see how He would heal and restore Halima's family. One of our team members was a former Hindu. Another, a former Buddhist, and another, a former Muslim. And Kathy, my precious wife, was a former cult member. God told me that He has anointed and appointed these four godly women to bring Halima and her family healing, restoration, and back to Jesus. He told me to immediately take this mighty foursome to their village. On the way, we fervently prayed for God's grace, favor, and wisdom.

Upon arrival, it was awkward. Pushing aside my uncertainties, I trusted God had spoken to me. I encouraged Kathy and our team to follow the Holy Spirit's guidance.

Kathy and our team ministered with much love and truth. It was a glorious time of healing and redemption. Halima and her family opened their hearts to receive the fullness of God's blessings. Everyone wept, laughed, and rejoiced as Kathy and our team shared their own trials, troubles, and persecutions. And how Jesus brought them comfort, healing, and restoration.

Wonderfully, our family returned to trusting Jesus amid their suffering and received prayers from Kathy and our team.

I had an impression of how they opened the door for demonic activity, and I was correct. Early on, I had cautioned Halima and her family about the dangers of practicing witchcraft. I told them they had to renounce such evil practices to receive God's grace, mercy, and cleansing. Moreover, I warned them that destruction could come to their house if they did not heed my advice (see Deuteronomy 7:26). I had a suspicion that a family member had not followed my advice and continued to engage in witchcraft.

I was correct. Someone in this clan continued practicing sorcery. The whole family allowed it, making them complicit in the wrongdoing. In Malaysia, I constantly pleaded with anyone who would listen not to engage in these pagan rituals. Witchcraft has been a practice and cancer to this beautiful nation for centuries.

Sadly, witchcraft is prevalent in our culture too. I'm alarmed how many Christian parents allow their children to play with Harry Potter games and other demonically inspired games.

Anwar battled thalassemia for ten years before passing. For unknown reasons, he only received partial healing. But Anwar lived much longer than his doctor's prognosis. Over the years, Anwar developed a special relationship with Jesus. Worship was his favorite pastime. When his time had come, Anwar was ready to meet Jesus. I'm excited to reunite with Anwar in heaven. To this day, Halima and her family remain close to us.

For example, never sacrifice your son or daughter as a burnt offering. And do not let your people practice fortune-telling, or use sorcery, or interpret omens, or engage in witchcraft, or cast spells, or function as mediums or psychics, or call forth the spirits of the dead. Anyone who does these things is detestable to the LORD. It is because the other nations have done these detestable things that the LORD your God will drive them out ahead of you (Deuteronomy 18:10-12 - NLT).

Reflections

The Good News was never meant to be a theory, philosophy, or religious allegory. Furthermore, the Good News was meant to be more than words but also demonstrations of miraculous signs and wonders. This has always been God's plan (see 1 Corinthians 2:1-5, 1 Thessalonians 1:5 & Acts 15:19).

Before I had the baptism of the Holy Spirit, my evangelism efforts had marginal success. However, after receiving this glorious baptism, my success in winning souls for Jesus exponentially increased.

Miraculous healings, casting out demons, prophetic words, and other miraculous signs and wonders were vital components to Jesus' ministry and to ours. Jesus came to set us free not only from sin but also from our infirmities and demonic torment. Compassion compelled Jesus to heal (see Matthew 9:35-37). It should be our motivation and pursuit as well.

Our healing ministry did not begin on the mission field in S.E. Asia but in Minnesota. We made it a practice to bring God's kingdom to the workplace, restaurants, malls, jails, and psychiatric wards. Wherever we saw an opportunity to be Christ's witnesses, we took a chance of looking foolish for Jesus. Those experiences prepared us for our international mission work.

Saad believed our message that Jesus is alive and heals. Our good news brought him hope. Our healing ministry was the seeds that brought salvation to him and his family.

God has given you spiritual gifts so that you can be a blessing to others. Don't let a spirit of intimidation keep you stuck (see 2 Timothy 1:6-8). Cry out to God for boldness and fan your gifts into flames. And don't worry about making mistakes. If love is your highest goal, Jesus will bring good from every one of your missteps. God is calling you to be His "change agent" everywhere and every day.

Threats From a Muslim Man
Changes Course

⁓⁓⁓

When friends from Minnesota came to visit us in Malaysia, we wanted them to experience Malaysian culture. Depending on their faith level, we provided different experiences for different friends. We brought those spiritually mature and bold in their faith to Muslim cities and villages to meet families we led to Jesus. Knowing threats loomed around each corner.

I wrote about how God led us to a Muslim fishing village through a vision in my previous story. And consequently, a clan of Muslims became Believers. This story is about Mohamed, Saad's oldest son we met under awkward circumstances a year prior. Saad warned us that Mohamed continually made threats to report his family to the Muslim religious police for converting to Christianity. Furthermore, Saad had a suspicion that his son had already informed the police about our Muslim evangelism. Hence, Saad's entire clan feared Mohamed would follow through with his threats, so they lived under a cloud of fear.

A married couple, and dear friends from Minnesota, came with us to meet several families we had led to Jesus. One of our stops was to meet Saad and his family. When we arrived, everyone greeted us with warm embraces. Saad and his family had adopted us. We dearly loved them. It was always a pleasure to spend time with this beautiful family despite the risks. Even though they were penniless, they always prepared a lavish feast for us! Love, honor, and respect were the foundation of our relationship.

Shortly after arriving, we all sat on the floor in the family living room. It was always a joyous reunion! As we got caught up with each other, suddenly, everyone got quiet -- fear suddenly swept through the room. Saad leaned over and whispered, "My son, Mohamed, just came, and he's sitting on the front porch, smoking a cigarette. He's eavesdropping on our conversations." Saad was terrified. He dearly loved his family and knew the Muslim religious police would severely persecute his family if his son reported them to the authorities.

I told Saad that I would go out to the porch, sit with his son, and have a talk with him. I reassured Saad everything would be okay. But I could see my words brought him little comfort.

It was an awkward moment, sitting down by Mohamed on the porch. Mohamed returned my warm greeting with a terse question, "Are you a Muslim?" His sarcasm provoked a long, intense response.

I replied, "You know I am not a Muslim, so I find it rude that you would ask me that. And I know why you are angry; your family are now Christians and followers of Jesus Christ. However, I want to make it very clear your family is now my family too, and there is nothing you can do to change that. My wife and I love your family with all our hearts, and we would do anything for them. If you think you must report us to the religious police, go and do it now. But it won't change the fact that we will always love your family." Mohamed was surprised by my candor and moved by my compassion for his family.

I went on to tell Mohamed about each family member and how I enjoyed their personalities. All the while I was pouring out my heart, he sat intently listening, smoking his cigarette. When I was finished talking, he respectfully thanked me and shook my hand.

Saad nervously watched the entire exchange from the entryway. Gratefully, my encounter with Mohamed calmed Saad. This story isn't done, though; it gets better.

On our next visit to see this clan, we brought a new disciple, Mabruk, a former Muslim, who we taught to be a missionary to his own people. We did not tell Mabruk any details about this clan except that they had converted to Christianity and were our disciples.

As we were all sitting on the floor, Mabruk asked Mohamed, who was sitting next to him, "Do you believe Jesus is the Son of God who came to save us from our sins?" Mabruk did not know that Mohamed had threatened his family and us. Overhearing their conversation, I was very curious how Mohamed would respond.

Mohamed boldly replied, "Yes, I believe Jesus is the Son of God.""Why do you believe," Mabruk pressed in. Mohamed took a deep breath and, with much conviction, replied, "I know my brothers, sisters, and their families well. Before they became Christians, they struggled with much contempt, jealousy, and bitterness towards one another. They were a miserable lot. Now, they show honor, respect, and dignity towards each other. Only God could make that happen. And they give all praise to Jesus their God for their transformation."

Hearing Mohamed's testimony, I was overcome with joy and gratitude. I'm thankful God encouraged me to speak to Mohamed on the porch!

Therefore, if anyone is in Christ, he is a new creation. The old has passed away; behold, the new has come (2 Corinthians 5:17 - ESV).

Reflections

On judgment day many, who believe they are Christians, will address Jesus as their Lord. Jesus' reply will be that He never knew them. Bewildered by Jesus' response, they will justify their Christian status by all their religious work. However, Jesus will remind them of their sinful lifestyle and tell them to go away. They will never enter the kingdom of heaven (see Matthew 7:21-23).

Praying the "sinners' prayer" does not get anyone saved. Only genuine faith in Jesus saves! And true faith always proves itself by its fruit. If a person is brought out of darkness into God's light, their transformed lives will demonstrate their repentance to be genuine. They will no longer be a slave to their sinful nature but be a slave to righteousness.

Initially, when Mohamed discovered his family became followers of Jesus, he was outraged. He threatened to report them and us to the religious police. Gratefully, God gave me the wisdom to shine understanding into Mohamed's heart. Consequently, Mohamed decided to be open-minded about their new religious beliefs.

Mohamed noticed that his family was no longer consumed by destructive behavior but showed each other's love, respect, gentleness, patience, and honor. Mohamed heard about several miracles in his family. However, that wasn't what changed his attitude towards Christianity. His family's remarkable transformation of character was what convinced him Jesus was God's Son. Mohamed wanted what they had and put his belief in Jesus.

Kathy's Seizure Leads a Buddhist to Salvation

‹‹

While we lived in Malaysia, we made friends from many different tribes. To this day, some of our closest friends are Malaysian. I enjoy my American roots and culture, but I identify more with Asian culture. It is rich in so many different facets. Perhaps God placed those seeds of desire in my heart to be an effective witness for Jesus to Asians.

Wu and Mia, a married Chinese couple, became close friends. They are first-generation Christians who converted from Buddhism when they were young. Wu and Mia knew we had extraordinary grace from God to successfully present Christ's gospel, no matter a person's religious background, personality, or skin color.

Concerned for the salvation of a friend's brother (Hai), Wu called to seek my advice. Hai was an accountant who followed Buddhism and strongly opposed Christianity. Hai also suffered from an incurable disease and debilitating depression. Wu deeply loved Hai and longed for him to know Jesus. Wu offered to pray for Hai, but Hai would have nothing to do with anything Christian. He was a stubborn Buddhist.

Wu's plan for Hai to hear the Good News involved us. He asked if we would be willing to meet with Hai, Mia, and himself for supper at a Chinese restaurant. We enthusiastically accepted his invitation. I told Wu, "On our first meeting with Hai, we will not attempt to overtly share the gospel; we will only take an interest in who he is as a person. If Hai does not trust the intentions of our heart, he will not trust our words." Wu agreed and acknowledged that was a prudent strategy.

The Chinese restaurant was right next to a Buddhist temple. That was

168

perfect; Hai would feel more at home and relaxed. Wu informed us that Hai was pragmatic and shy, making it difficult to engage in conversation. Kathy and I enjoy and take delight in all personalities. Hai's shyness would not be a hindrance.

After introductions, we asked Hai many questions about his interests and found him intelligent, knowledgeable, and engaging. We had an enjoyable time with Hai. It was apparent the feelings were mutual. We were careful to show no other agenda than love.

Hai opened his heart and shared about his illness and how it horribly impacted his life. However, we discerned it would not be appropriate to offer prayers. Hai would see it as a setup and betrayal of trust. It was best to be a good ear. So we listened and showed Hai much compassion.

When we departed, Hai let us know that he really enjoyed fellowship with us. We told him we felt the same. By faith, we believed God would open Hai's heart to receive prayers from us sometime later. We just needed to be patient and not pushy. And so, it happened!

Later, I received a call from my friend Wu. He said, "Hai's condition has worsened; he is nearing death. Needing a miracle, I implored Hai to open his heart for prayers. Hai relented and said he would only allow Mark and Kathy to pray for him. Mark, would you and Kathy go to Hai's residence and pray for Jesus to heal him." "Of course," I replied.

Upon arrival, Hai appeared scared and depressed. He desperately needed a touch from Jesus. Kathy and I have experienced countless similar moments; they are always heartbreaking. We mourned with Hai. However, we did not allow him to stay in a place of pity. Jesus is the answer for all our troubles. Jesus is Hai's hope and peace!

Hai was expecting prayers, and that was a good thing. But he needed more than physical healing. Hai needed eternal healing, and I would not deny him that opportunity. I said to Hai, "We will pray that Jesus heals you. But before we pray, can I share about my relationship with Jesus?" "Yes," he replied respectfully.

Jesus and His crucifixion mean everything to me. Whenever I share the "Good News," I am overcome with love for my Lord. This was no exception. Hai saw that my relationship with Jesus was not theoretical but authentic and tender. Hai carefully hung on my every word. Then something bizarre happened.

Kathy was sitting nearby. While I was sharing with Hai, Kathy suddenly cried out, "Mark, I am not feeling well." She was frightened and looked pale. Then Kathy started to violently shake; she was having a seizure. Kathy fell out of her chair onto the floor and continued to shake. I shouted, "Someone call for an ambulance." I checked to see if she was breathing; she appeared not to be. I was terrified. I didn't know how to minister CPR and hoped someone present did.

Then, suddenly, Kathy opened her eyes and started to breathe again. To begin with, she was disoriented, not knowing what had happened to her. After getting her bearings back, I told her I would immediately take her to the hospital. Kathy strongly resisted. "Mark, you have not fully shared the "Good News" with Hai. And we have not prayed for his healing. We will go nowhere until both happen," she emphatically stated.

Hai was shocked by Kathy's demeanor and proclamation. With sincerity, he responded, "Kathy, there is no need for Mark to talk any further. Your compassion for me to know Jesus, despite your seizure, convinced me Jesus is real. I am ready to surrender my life to Jesus as my Lord and Savior; please pray for me." What an unbelievable, tender, and priceless moment.

Hai received Jesus, and we prayed for his healing. We all celebrated and rejoiced over Hai's new birth. Hai stated that he had never felt genuine peace until surrendering his life to Jesus. Kathy's health dramatically improved, giving me peace. Our time with Hai ended on a glorious note!

A few months later, I received another call from my good friend, Hu. He said, "Mark, Hai departed from this life and is now with Jesus. He did not get physically healed, but we all know Hai has a new body like an Angel's and is now in heaven. Also, we noticed that Hai remained peaceful, even the day he passed. We had never seen him happier. Thank you and Kathy for being his friend."

He will take our weak mortal bodies and change them into glorious bodies like his own, using the same power with which he will bring everything under his control (Ephesians 3:21 -NLT).

Reflections

Gentleness is a powerful weapon to destroy demonic strongholds. Hai was a "bruised reed" who could easily break (see Matthew 12:20). Hai had a lonely life; he carefully sheltered himself from being criticized or rejected by others. Hai desired to have a relationship with us because he deemed us to be safe. We never pushed Jesus onto Hai.

Showing Hai extraordinary gentleness and patience was God's plan to remove the veil of deception from Hai so that he could clearly see Jesus. We honored Hai by taking a keen interest in his life. Hai knew that we genuinely enjoyed his personality.

When Hai was confronted with imminent death, he became fearful. Gratefully, Hai trusted us for prayers. Kathy's love for Hai was proven sincere when she refused to go to the hospital after having a seizure. She demonstrated she cared more for Hai's wellbeing than her own. Our actions will show others if our faith is genuine or not.

Love must be our highest goal when witnessing God's truth and power to others. When a person trusts your heart, they are more inclined to trust your words. Many Muslims have told us that the miracles opened their eyes, but our crazy, unconditional love convinced them that Jesus is God's Son.

Buddhist's Grandson is Delivered from Agoraphobia

The first house we rented in Malaysia had no air conditioners. It was a challenge adjusting to Malaysia's tropical climate. Especially coming from Minnesota. Malaysia's hot and humid climate caused us to be continuously drenched in sweat. Looking for a measure of relief, I hired a Chinese plumber (Wang Wei) to install several air conditioners in our house. Wang Wei was a proud Buddhist.

After completing the project, I paid Wang Wei for his work. Then unexpectedly, I was compelled to give him my ministry card and share an impression. I proclaimed, "I could be wrong, but I am sensing an evil spirit will be tormenting you in the future. And if that happens, and you find no way to expel the demon, call me. My God has given me authority over all the power of evil spirits. If what I say happens, call me, and I will banish the evil spirit in Jesus' Name."

Buddhists are spiritually sensitive; they believe evil spirits exist. Moreover, exorcism is a common Monk practice. Thus, Wang Wei considered my forewarning credible, took my card, and placed it in his wallet.

Six years later, Wang Wei called me on the phone. To begin with, I could not remember Wang Wei or the conversation I had with him. From when he installed our air conditioners till six years later, Kathy and I had prayed for thousands of people. But as Wang Wei continued to talk, I remembered him and the impression I gave him.

Wang Wei stated he had placed my ministry card in his wallet, forgetting about it until recently. He informed me that my perception of a tormenting demon came about six years earlier. An evil spirit tormented his grandson,

Lei Wei. Desperate to find deliverance, Wang Wei heard a voice, "Call the American pastor; he will know what to do. His ministry card is still in your wallet." Wang Wei looked in his wallet, and sure enough, there was my ministry card. Wang Wei begged me to free his grandson from the demon. He said, "The evil spirit relentlessly torments my grandson day and night. The evil spirit tells him tragedy will come upon him if he leaves his house." Phycologists have labeled the irrational fear of leaving home or entering crowded spaces agoraphobia. Consequently, Lie Wei, who was ten years old, refused to attend school. Sadly, his grades were failing.

It was apparent Wang Wei loved his grandson dearly. Though he didn't have to, Wang Wei kept persisting that I help his grandson. Our schedule was packed full; nevertheless, compassion compelled me to make time for his grandson's deliverance early the following day. I told Wang Wei to bring his grandson to my house and that in the Name of Jesus, his grandson would find freedom. As if I did not understand his concerns, he replied, "Pastor, didn't you hear me? My grandson refuses to leave the house. He's terrified to do so!" I gently responded, "Yes, I heard you. But I'm going to pray that God gives your grandson momentary freedom from that tormenting spirit. God wants to encourage you both by giving your grandson strength. Call me back if I am wrong, and I will go to where Lie Wei is staying."

God answered my prayer; both grandfather and grandson showed up at our front door early the following day. Lie Wei was a delightful child, well-mannered and gentle in spirit. Lie Wei told me that the demon constantly said that he would die a horrible death if he left his house.

I shared many testimonies about Jesus. Also, I shared how Jesus had set me free from irrational fears, including claustrophobia. Finally, I shared how God used Kathy and me to release many people from demonic torment, including a young Hindu man (David) who was also tormented by a spirit of agoraphobia. When we first met David, he told us fear had imprisoned him in his house for five years. David gave his life to Jesus, was set free, and the evil spirit never tormented him again. Shortly after his deliverance, David moved to another state and enjoyed life to its fullest in Jesus Christ. Both Wang Wei and Lie Wei were profoundly encouraged by my testimonies and the Good News of salvation.

The Holy Spirit prompted me to ask them if they believed Jesus was God's Son and that my testimonies were true. They both acknowledged their belief. Encouraged by their response, I stated, "Jesus will save anyone who surrenders their lives to His Lordship. Moreover, Jesus will make a home in their hearts, and they will have fellowship with Him forever. Also, they will possess His authority over all the power of darkness. And God will give them immeasurable grace, peace, joy. And God will help them live virtuous and productive lives. Best of all, God's children will experience His loving kindness forever."

Wang Wei and his grandson needed no further encouragement. With tears streaming down their cheeks and holding each other's hand, grandfather and grandson confessed their sins, received forgiveness, and asked Jesus into their hearts to be their Lord and Savior. Then, in the mighty Name of Jesus, I commanded the evil spirit to leave Lie Wei. It was a glorious moment; Jesus instantly set him free.

Lie Wei's countenance swiftly changed from gloom to glee. That glorious day, Jesus destroyed the works of the devil in his life. And both grandfather and grandson were reborn into a new creation. And all of Heaven celebrated!

Lie Wei could not stop smiling. With exuberance, he exclaimed, "I know the evil spirit has left me; I am no longer afraid." Lie Wei found inexpressible freedom in Jesus. And with broad smiles, both grandfather and grandson praised Jesus for His unfailing mercy.

I asked Wang Wei if he knew of a Chinese Christian church they could attend. I told him it was vital for them to belong to a Christian fellowship for their faith to grow. Wang Wei replied, "A close friend of mine, who is Christian, keeps inviting me to his church. I am now eager to do so with my grandson.

The Holy Spirit prompted me to give my ministry card to a Chinese plumber and share a word of knowledge. The seed I planted brought salvation to a Buddhist plumber and his grandson six years later. I'm glad I obeyed that prompting from the Holy Spirit.

And Jesus rebuked the demon, and it came out of him, and the boy was healed instantly (Matthew 17:18 ESV).

Reflections

A sudden thought, urge, or intuition may be part of God's plans. The Holy Spirit can be the source of those promptings. Many biblical examples support my premise. The Holy Spirit compelled Jesus to go into the wilderness for 40 days (see Mark 1:12). Paul was compelled to make a sudden trip to Macedonia to preach (see Acts 19:11). The Lord inspired the kings of the Medes to march against Babylon (see Jeremiah 51:11). And there are multitudes of other biblical examples.

When we allow Holy Spirit to lead our lives, promptings can initiate "words of knowledge," "prophetic utterances," or "words of wisdom." I have experienced all the above.

In contrast, when we allow the desires of our flesh to lead our lives, we give access to demonic promptings. Satan prompted Judas to betray Jesus (see John 13:2). God allowed a demonic spirit to inspire all of King Ahab's prophets to speak lies (see 1 King 22:22).

Therefore, loving God and people must be our highest goal. If we allow pride, idolatry, our bitterness to take root in our souls, we will be in danger of being prompted by the wrong spirit. Jesus rebuked James and John after they wanted to call down fire from heaven to destroy a city that rejected their ministry.

But He turned and rebuked them, and said, "You do not know what manner of spirit you are of. For the Son of Man did not come to destroy men's lives but to save them (Luke 9:55-56 NKJV)."

I had a prompting to warn the Chinese plumber that he would encounter a tormenting demon in the future. I am so glad I did. It brought salvation and freedom to him and his grandson. It was a priceless and glorious moment.

If you allow compassion for others to be your highest goal, the Holy Spirit will prompt you to act on your compassion. You will be compelled to bring a "word of encouragement," an "act of kindness," or some other blessing from God. God gives promptings to those who walk in mercy rather than judgment. God trusts they will represent Him well!

Made in the USA
Monee, IL
28 April 2022

95006504R00105